METAL MEN

METAL MEN

MARC RICH AND THE 10-BILLION-DOLLAR SCAM

A. CRAIG COPETAS

HARRAP · LONDON

First published in Great Britain 1986
by HARRAP LIMITED
19–23 Ludgate Hill, London EC4M 7PD

First published by G. P. Putnam's Sons, 1985

ISBN 0 245-54406-2

Printed and bound in Great Britain
by Billings Ltd, Worcester

FOR
B.D.
DON ERICKSON
&
MARGARET SAGAN

CONTENTS

PROLOGUE

White knights shine too brightly on the battlefield. They get knocked off too easily.

LEE MARVIN

I T WOULD HAVE BEEN impossible to write from the outside about fugitive American trader Marc Rich and the men who absolutely control the market for the Earth's natural resources. Beyond the unique experience of living and working among metal traders, the secretive nature of their lives necessitated my physically becoming a trader. I went inside and spent a year observing their profession as a working trader with international bankers, ship owners, oil dealers, commodity traders, exchange brokers and mining executives.

I bargained for tungsten and cadmium in China; negotiated the establishment of shadowy offshore companies in Switzerland, the Cayman Islands, Panama and the Netherlands Antilles. When the war between Iran and Iraq reached fever pitch in 1984, I assisted in brokering oil cargoes on the Red Sea and fielded daily reports from the Kharg Island petroleum terminals off the Iranian coast. On occasion I found myself being directed to trade Midwestern corn for African cobalt or haggling for the rights to a British fish farm in return for a piece of action on a $1 million deal for a metal called ferro vanadium. Anything . . . any deal was possible.

9

The pace of a trader is nonstop. As a junior trader at one of the London trading houses where I worked, I had to arise daily at 5 A.M. to review the overnight telex traffic from Hong Kong and Singapore to see whether or not there was any Far Eastern market action to be taken advantage of before dawn rose on the Western world. To ensure that I got out of bed on time, a telex machine was installed next to my bedroom and the incoming bell was turned up to its highest volume.

On a trip to the Dutch port of Rotterdam, I was ferried by skiff through twelve miles of choppy North Sea swells to a cargo ship hauling iron ore that apparently belonged to Marc Rich. Once in port I helped off-load the loose ore buried in the ship's hold. Days were spent exploring and working in Rotterdam's vast complex of metal warehouses and oil terminals. At one point I was flown by helicopter to meet with sources on an oil tanker speeding into port, lowered onto the moving supership through English Channel crosswinds by harness.

In the Soviet Union Western traders allowed me to accompany them into Russian corporate suites to observe firsthand how politically sensitive deals were structured. A few hours before I was to step onto a plane to China with a London metal trader who had made me his apprentice, another multimillion-dollar deal transpired in Chicago, forcing him to fly west, as I sped east with directives to negotiate for millions of dollars' worth of Chinese metal. "Just do everything I told you," the trader advised as he put me in a car to London's Gatwick Airport. "A solo experience will make you understand the edge we live on."

Another key reason why I became a trader was that Marc Rich refused all requests to be interviewed, making it critical to enter his world so that I might get as close to the man as possible.

Marc Rich is known as a metal trader, but he deals, like all metal traders, in whatever products come out of the Earth—metal, oil, gas, grain. To watch the metal men trade is to view a particular business phenomenon: men, who by virtue of their wits, are able to operate as powerful and uncontested freelance salesmen of the Earth's resources. Originally, metal men dealt solely in metal. But as times changed, so did the metal men, and their markets grew to include anything buried or sown in the Earth. Although a metal man might make more money from a particular oil or grain deal, he is still known as a metal man because trading metal is the foundation of his business. No matter the material traded, the conundrum is how to make money out of whatever the Earth has to offer.

Marc Rich is their greatest money-maker. Right now he is in self-proclaimed exile in Switzerland, remaining there to avoid federal warrants for his arrest in the largest criminal scheme to evade taxes in American history. Under the open protection of the Swiss government, his various companies are still trading over $12 billion worth of metal, oil and other commodities in America and around the world.

I first collided with Marc Rich in the summer of 1982 in his penthouse office in Manhattan's Piaget Building. The occasion was entirely coincidental: I had friends in the trading business, and we had arranged to meet some people who worked at Marc Rich International, Rich's American company. Marc Rich entered the office lobby as we were about to board an elevator. "That's Marc Rich," said one of the traders. "They say he's worth $10 billion."

The meeting would have remained forgettable, except that one year later Marc Rich was slapped with a fifty-one-count federal indictment on a host of criminal conspiracy charges, transforming the $10 billion man I had seen in a lobby into the most wanted white-collar criminal in America. I began asking questions and before too long discovered that the personal and corporate character of Marc Rich provided a unique opportunity to observe what happens when money—real money—goes berserk.

I became a metal trader on December 1, 1983. My friends and acquaintances in the trading profession provided the necessary introductions and, on occasion, cover stories to explain my presence within the metal world. Over 200 people with knowledge of Marc Rich, his far-flung financial interests and personal habits were interviewed. No one was quoted on Marc Rich without prior knowledge. Many of these men would not cooperate unless their anonymity was guaranteed. One of the reasons for their request was that Marc Rich still owed them money; others were frightened of what Rich might do to anyone who appeared disloyal to his empire in the wake of a massive federal investigation into his personal activities and business practices. Rich was obviously an incredibly powerful man.

I never spoke with Marc Rich, but I did collide with him again at high noon, March 12, 1984, in the tiny Swiss canton of Zug. He was on the lam.

I had followed the instructions of an inside source and waited in the lobby of his international corporate headquarters high rise. He slid anonymously out of one of the elevators and down a snow-dusted street past a vacant lot into a Swiss pizza joint dolled up to resemble a classy Italian restaurant. I stalked him to the restaurant and waited until he had entered. He was greeted immediately by the owner and ushered quickly to a table in the back corner. But before Rich settled into the wooden chair to lunch with his business partner, Pinky Green, his dark eyes coolly scanned the dining area, like Butch Cassidy searching for the Pinkerton Boys. Finally satisfied he would be alone with Green, he sat down, his back against the wall and with a clear view of the comings and goings of the lunchtime crowd.

I took a table nearby and watched. Rich was quite tall, with spidery legs, sinewy fingers, a St. Moritz tan and absolutely no trace of a smile. On sight it was strikingly clear that what I had been told about Marc Rich was true. His physical presence was commanding, and it was easy to understand why he was a force majeure in the multibillion-dollar commodity business. Many traders actually trembled when his name was mentioned; all of them assured me that Rich was a man who would gamble his life if the financial reward were high enough. Sitting there in a jet black suit at a safe remove from the federal posse in New York City trying to extradite him back to the United States, he certainly dressed the part of an executive outlaw.

Soon after his arrival, a waiter sped up with a steaming plate of pasta and a glass of ruby red wine, whereupon Rich began to roll his hands together like a child about to dive into his favorite food. After a few zestily devoured forkfuls, he stood up and started towards the bathroom. It seemed like the only shot I would have at meeting Rich *mano a mano* and without having to deal with Green and the other guys who hovered constantly around him like worker bees attending their queen. The dining area was reasonably empty, so when he walked by me I stood up and said calmly, "Mr. Rich . . . ," but I never finished. He looked at me, frightened, his chill brown eyes flashing the agony of ripped flesh. Hunching over, he bounded quickly through the kitchen and then backtracked slightly to reach the bathroom. Marc Rich, the man whom the United States Justice Department privately called the most corrupt corporate executive in America, never returned to finish his lunch. He was gone. Marc Rich, king of the commodity cowboys, had heaved himself through the washroom window of a Zug pizzeria to avoid comment, leaving his blue cashmere overcoat, a Florentine leather briefcase and an unfinished lunch of capellini d'angelo and filetto al pomodoro on the table with Pinky Green. What you will read is the story of the man who escaped through that bathroom window and of the world he leapt into.

PART I
MINERAL RITES

CHAPTER 1

"See here old bean," the consul heard himself saying, "to have against you Franco, or Hitler, is one thing, but to have Actinium, Argon, Beryllium, Dysprosium, Niobium, Palladium, Praseodymium, Ruthenium, Samarium, Silicon, Tantalum, Tellurium, Terbium, Thorium, Thulium, Titanium, Uranium, Vanadium, Virginium, Xenon, Ytterbium, Yttrium, Zirconium, to say nothing of Europium and Germanium—ahip!—and Columbium!—against you, and all the others, is another."

MALCOLM LOWRY, *Under the Volcano*

CITY OF LONDON, core of the industrial trading world, had fallen prey to a damp North Sea winter. Numbing Arctic winds, gathering the bitter damp as they blasted south across the Norfolk Broads, burrowed through the mist of schemes to buy and sell the Earth's crust like mud worms, sending London's metal traders in search of the nearest bottle of bonded bourbon. They all needed a drink. The big money these guys liked to roll for had surrendered to the weather and stayed frozen. The strength of the 1984 Ronald Wilson Reagan dollar was growing daily against all foreign currencies, causing fiscal headaches for traders acquiring dollars with devalued Eurocurrencies in order to buy metal contracted to be purchased in dollars. It was a preposterous situation.

Trader Robbins called it gout season—the time of year when industrial doges discussed the effects of ballooning cobalt prices with struggling African economic ministers over glass after glass of French Grand Cru poured by the waiters at Langan's Brasserie in Mayfair. The expense accounts were working overtime, every senior trader in town putting at least

17

one afternoon aside to court a fresh banker and crank up a bank line. Pubs in the City overflowed with junior varsity traders dispatched to slosh up commodity market floor brokers with enormous jars of Guinness and doughy pub sausages slathered in steak sauce. All the metal men were on the prowl, looking for the next swizzle, the next hot metal that could be bought, sold or sacrificed to bring some life back into the torpid market.

"We metal traders are jugglers without arms," Robbins declared, bored over his second pint of afternoon lager and the small $5,000 realized that morning selling Russian rhodium, the most expensive of the platinum-based metals, to an American who would probably sell it for use in the construction of an American cruise missile guidance system. "We make money out of disasters. Disruption compels people to run for cover. We provide that cover. But it is essential that you never believe everything you hear from a metal trader because he will only tell you what it suits his current inventory to tell you.

"Our business is the sharp end of what's taking place in the capitalist system," Trader Robbins added, removing his glasses and pushing four fingers through his curly black hair. "The public forgets that every industry in the world is metal-oriented. We control the metal. There are even a few traders who could make a go at controlling the world."

There are ten commodity markets in the United States, dozens more overseas. They are places where dealings in a particular item are made and recorded on a national or international scale. Historically, London has long been the home of most commodity exchanges even though, in modern times, the transactions are no longer in the physical goods themselves, but in paper dealings for possession of title. The process is facilitated by grading systems that save the trouble of personal inspection. Commodities like metal can be bought, shipped and sold without the person effecting the transaction ever setting eyes on the material. Dealings can be spot—at the current price—or future—at an agreed price that will not be affected by movements in the spot price prior to the date on which the future transaction is scheduled to be completed. London's geographical position is advantageous to this process because it allows traders to conduct arbitrage deals, heavy-mannered gambles where a trader scoops metal in one market and then sells and ships it into another market where the price of the same material is higher. Arbitragers sense and swoop. It is said they are born with a sixth sense for market distortions. Time differences grace London's arbitragers, permitting them, for example, to buy something from a Far Eastern market for a dollar in the morning and then turn around and sell it to a North American customer or exchange for two dollars, while the Far East is getting ready for bed.

Every exchange broker requires a special license to deal within the pit, but metal traders need no official stamp of approval. And it is within this theater, far above the blood-curdling spasms of the world's commodity brokerage pits, light-years removed from Madison Avenue commercials extolling the virtues of municipal bond portfolios, that the heavy money is made, the real power executed. But ask any twenty metal traders what a commodity is and you'll be waist deep in economic rhetoric. Even seasoned trading executives have a difficult time defining what it is they do. Amplify the problem these traders have in agreeing on a job description and it becomes much easier to understand why the majority of the public gets burned when they start to play the commodity markets with hedged promises of big returns on small investments. "Commodity trading," warned a senior executive at the multinational metal-trading firm Bomar Resources, "was made to seem extremely special and complicated to protect the interests of the people involved. To play these markets you had better be extremely smart, stupid or wealthy."

"We sell the ingredients necessary for industry," stressed metal man Frank Wolstencroft, president of Cambridge Metals, a London–New York trading firm that specializes in nickel for steel, rhodium for catalytic converters in automobiles and tungsten for light bulb filaments. "We can also sell greed. Greed can be just as profitable."

Metal traders are the undisputed high priests of the commodity world, and their liturgy is one of unadulterated risk. Unlike the commodity dealer from a brokerage house who spends his days exercising the financial whims of others, the metal trader forges his own markets in whatever the Earth has to offer. He will furnish metal to be brokered on an exchange, but he also reserves the ability to shatter an exchange by the uncontrolled application or retention of his wares to the controlled market. Many traders have the bankroll to maintain personal floor brokers who can, on occasion, bewitch a commodity market by prudently juggling their wares between exchanges and wealthy freelance punters. Most metals, however, aren't even traded on exchanges but move through smooth private transactions among a clique of old-line dealers. "You're under the protection of no rules or regulations when dealing with many metals," said E. F. Andrews, a vice president of Allegheny International. "You're on the fringe of the market at best."

Breaking the metal bank is not easy, and most would find it simpler to beat the house at a chemin de fer table in Monte Carlo. There is a winner and a loser in every trade. It is a mean game, a zero-sum game, and the metal man is always the winner because, unlike the private investor, he controls the market he plays. He plays both sides: He's a buyer when he thinks the market will go up; a seller when he thinks the market will go down.

This independence and virtual freedom from regulation have made metal traders an oppressively clandestine group of individuals who generate trillions of dollars by quietly controlling the buying and selling of the Earth's crust. Metal traders will joke that on a slow day they relieve boredom by "common exchange gambling" on grain and pig bellies; nevertheless their profit and power come from the influence they wield buying, selling and supplying the Earth's geology to industry and individuals. The drama of their lives is directed by the cost and the availability of metals like copper, tin and tantalum, and by ocean ships stuffed with fossil fuels and strange-sounding lumps of earth called ferro molybdenum, wolfram trioxide and chambishi cobalt. Their edge on life is a canny understanding and utilization of the labyrinthine complexities of tax loopholes and exotic financial havens in places such as Panama, Liberia and Switzerland.

Of the eighty naturally occurring metals buried in the Earth, forty are of critical industrial importance. Only nine of these metals—which the metal men supply uniquely—are openly brokered and monitored on exchanges; the rest are dealt under the absolute control of the metal-trading community. The majority of these metals come from politically volatile countries like South Africa, Zambia and Zaire, sparking fears among American politicians that the Soviet Union—which is self-sufficient in minerals—has a policy of tempting these nations to sever their supply lines to American industry.

The metal trader, however, perceives these rocks as casino chips of varying costs to be gambled immediately or tucked away in a warehouse to gather dust until the odds are stacked in his favor. Like a major corporation that might direct a division to purchase a piece of an Atlantic City casino, an investment outfit like Merrill-Lynch, Shearson Lehman American Express or Smith Barney directs its subsidiaries to deal in various metal markets on behalf of their clients. But metal trading is a virtuoso business where an individual trader, like a pit boss, can easily exert more power than the company that employs him. And every metal trader has an electric streak of outlaw in him. It comes with the territory. Outlaw bravado is a by-product of the tense thrill these men experience from making and losing millions of dollars in a matter of moments; any metal man who has experienced the wired sensation of a million-dollar profit from one phone call would quickly agree that making such big money in so short a time is turbocharged with larcenous excitement. "It is a business for independent souls," said William May, a member of the board of Phibro-Salomon, the holding company that owns Philipp Brothers, the world's largest and most powerful metal-trading juggernaut. "Metal traders have a built-in talent to sense opportunities that other businessmen cannot see. Traders are a bunch of cowboys, highly individualistic and generally adding little to an organization as a whole."

The esoteric nature of the metal business makes it an industry open to all kinds of prostitution. In 1981, for example, United States agents busted the Wall Street headquarters of Mineral Resources Incorporated, a boiler-room operation huckstering tantalum, a strategic and precious metal used to make sophisticated electronic equipment. Over thirty traders were indicted on fraud and grand larceny charges of ripping off some $1.3 million from 144 unwary investors.

The scam was geared for greed: Mineral Resources was selling tantalum to the public for $400 a pound when the free-market price was little more than $90 a pound. The traders, nonetheless, promised returns of 300 and 400 percent, while neglecting to inform their clients that their tantalum scrap was too inferior to be used industrially. Although Mineral Resources was a phone-bank operation playing on the unsophisticated investor, the eminent pursuit of industrial trading is just as open to brigandage. It all depends on the trader.

Individuality in corporate life may be cultivated in public, as economist John Kenneth Galbraith once pointed out, but should an executive reach the inner sanctums of corporate power and accept an invitation to appear in a video bite with Dan Rather, the individualistic leader will transform himself into another cog in the organization. With rare exception, the personalities of these executives, Galbraith believes, are lost, sometimes without notice, for the overall good of the corporation.

Metal trading is the exception to the rule. Metal traders are loners, and their personalities are involved intimately with

22

every aspect of their professional life. Nearly all of their trad-ing offices are decorated with blowups of the periodic table of the elements. They will smirk and tell you that such art eclipses their business activities; one look reminds most vis-itors of tedious hours spent staring at high school chemistry class walls, memorizing atomic structure and molecular weight. The metal men use the table as a high technology tote board. They shoot as high as any professional gambler can. They win more often than they lose. Their vigorish comes from one part experience to nine parts pugnacity, and their ability to trade is entirely automatic. As a group they are formidable. Their ranks reward old pros and hot-shot kids with equal shares; they grapple for kaleidoscopic power in an arena that they alone control, bellicose gamesters who anywhere else would have been banned from the casino.

Marc Rich was one of those who took a shot at controlling the game. He was much more than a commodity trader; he was the Metal Man, the grand dragon of a daring and tightly knit lodge of 2,000 men described bravely as "barbarians" by London Metal Exchange Chairman Michael Brown. Rich was the most successful, intimidating and, says the United States government, corrupt member of this international fraternity, the man called El Matador because of his refined talent and enthusiasm in killing bull markets when they did not suit the designs of his global empire. "Ruthless tycoon," "vengeful businessman" and "scheming marketeer" were a few of the ways colleagues described his towering personality. Those traders who have found themselves on the short end of a Rich deal have called him greedy, wicked, amoral and a mutineer. Traders who worked alongside Rich say he was an egotistical genius, a beautifully sinister executive who could frame deals with the artistry of a pool shark. The metal men were awed by Marc Rich, the man who took pleasure in being billed as the lonely and deserted trader who never made it through college, the autocrat who hired outcasts, yet wandered corporate corridors to steal the competition's cream and transform them ultimately into the Los Angeles Raiders of professional trading.

Marc Rich was the apotheosis of a blood-and-guts trader, a financial gladiator whose interest rested in the spoils of battle. Within seven short years Rich masterminded a $15-billion-a-year trading business by specializing in metal, inventing spot oil, dabbling in grain, sugar and weapons. In the process he assumed 50 percent ownership of Twentieth Century-Fox and bought an oil refinery in Guam that sold Iranian petroleum to fuel the United States Seventh Fleet. He enjoyed eating, so he built one of Switzerland's most expensive and glittery restaurants across the street from his Zug headquarters. He gobbled up real estate like so many after-dinner mints. He bullied the currency markets, pitting the price of today's dollar against what it might be three months, or three hours, hence.

Marc Rich—the man whom secretaries called the "Rudolph Valentino" of the commodity industry—had the jazz, the ability to create and exploit what commodity dealers called "the profitable commodity situation." He remained the most secretive of all metal merchants, preferring to exile himself and his family to Switzerland and pay over sixteen months' worth of contempt of court fines at a daily rate of $50,000 rather than relinquish corporate records that could send him to jail for over 300 years.

He has spent his entire life cutting deals, speculating on nearly any item with a price tag on the world market. Slybooting metals like the Artful Dodger, he risked billions to seize control of large caches of strategic commodities. Marc Rich understood the madness of crowds and how to choreograph their delusions to enrich his empire. Nothing was sacred in the Marc Rich organization; that was a cliché elevated to corporate scripture.

Rich was what the French called *rastaquouère*, a member of a nobility born from fat wallets, not blood. It was a royalty of monetary might, and Rich was its undisputed king. His court was treated well. He would pay twenty-five-year-old traders $85,000 a year, with huge performance bonuses snuggled safely away from the tax man's grasp in offshore accounts. He was the executive who never fired an employee, deducing it better to cast off the unwanted with quarterly cash payments to ensure their silence on the inner workings of his business. But above the measures of money paid to Rich's finely tuned staff, risky business was encouraged, individuality generously rewarded. "Rich rarely complained when his traders lost money," said one of his metal men, "because he knew that was the best way to train traders how to make massive amounts of money."

Marc Rich's brand of business was not offered in the Harvard Business School prospectus, and he disdained the prospect of holding himself accountable to the 7 o'clock news or the editorial page of the *Wall Street Journal*. It was a commerce conducted in shadows, its characters motivated by heady drives that could, at any moment, career out of control. The high was everlasting in the corporate suites of Marc Rich, but the metabolization of such power sometimes ended in death for traders ordered to exceed the limits of their own avaricious personalities.

Rich knew about the velocity of money, about keeping cash in a state of perpetual motion in the world's financial markets in order to generate more money. He knew that no government would have an easy time nailing down his billions when the money was telegraphed into bank accounts for as little as twenty-four hours to take advantage of a one-quarter percent interest hike before being transferred to another financial institution that offered his billions a better deal. Those who know Rich joke that lists of the world's wealthiest men exclude his name because they have no formula with which to gauge his total worth. And even if the government had a treasure map to his domestic fortune there would be no way to design taxes or laws to totally muzzle his operations in Southeast Asia, the Caribbean, the Middle East, Latin Amer-

A. *CRAIG COPETAS*

ica, the Soviet Union, Europe, China. Marc Rich, say those who know him, would make a pact with the devil if he could become a cartel.

A trader's profits are supposed to be the result of a quality of things in relation to the desires and needs of men. But more often than not, the creation of a market is little more than psychical image making, a conjuring technique that actually dates back to 1559, when Konrad Gesner, a wandering European merchant, stumbled across a garden of blooming tulips in Germany and sparked tulipomania. The tulip did absolutely nothing, served no industrial or medical purpose and held no imagined magical properties. It was, in fact, a totally expendable item. But tulipomania ran through Europe faster than a fourteenth-century rat carried plague because merchants convinced themselves and the public that tulips were worthwhile investments.

By 1636 the tulip situation had grown out of control. Tulip stock markets were established throughout Europe, with the most influential of them situated in the Netherland port towns where consignments were off-loaded and warehoused. But before calm could be restored, the speculators set off fluctuations in tulip futures that sent the cost of a single well-formed bulb upwards of $100,000. The public started betting on what the price and quality of next week's tulip shipments would be, and shiploads of tulips were kept floating offshore until traders forced up their price.

A baffling code of tulip trading laws was drawn up, and professional tulip investigators were empowered to enforce them throughout Europe. The tulip police were, by an accident of history, the world's first Securities and Exchange Commission, complete with a complicated bureaucracy of red tape to monitor the way in which shady dealers brokered tulip futures. The lawmakers failed miserably; nothing could contain the economic fury associated with the tulip, and tulipomania soon became a gross caricature of the economic system.

The dynamics of tulipomania were, of course, little more

than mental tricks that catered to a public still in the throes of establishing the intricacies of a sophisticated market structure. But when the dust settled, no dealer knew exactly how many tulips there were and no government had any idea of how to regulate this new breed of trader. Today the business of international trade is computerized, clarified and often classified, yet the techniques behind the creation of tulipomania are still used to shatter entire marketplaces in one devastating burst of free enterprise.

Commodities, metals or otherwise, are more than items necessary for everyday life—they are a condition, a state of mind. And what metal traders do is sympathetically create manicured images around simple objects of trade. The public impression of a commodity is, by and large, more important in determining the item's price than is its real industrial value. Incalculable profit is the upside and financial disaster the downside of such manipulative knowledge for the world's two thousand metal men. Magnates can be made, or criminals can be packed off to jail. Where a metal man ends up hinges largely on how much risk he decides to take, how much bilious panic he wishes to create. The lessons to the modern trader are: On the one hand, consider any trick to control a commodity and, on the other hand, make sure you can get away with it.

The science of economics has a principle called the Law of Diminishing Marginal Utility, a high-priced translation of the old street maxim "Too much of anything will end up killing you real dead." Diminishing marginal utility has a way of popping up in times of great commercial prosperity. In good times people have a tendency to overspeculate on what the market has to offer. They take exaggerated chances, do everything possible to be in on a quick-kill scheme—and metal dealing is guerrilla economics of the highest order: behind-the-lines business, in and out. Fast.

Rich did the unexpected for the sheer joy of seeing if he could get away undetected. He played by his own rules because the standard rules did not give him access to the deal-making power he craved. He went to great pains to look the part of a boilerplated corporate executive, but beneath the handmade shirts and finely woven silk ties pumped the blood of a wildcat. Behind the computer-key-locked doors of his expensively decorated offices in Manhattan, Zug and forty other locations around the world resided a stable of rowdy businessmen, handpicked by Rich because he knew the money they could generate if none of the usual rules applied. Rich's style drilled holes through whatever ethical constraints and business disciplines girdled the competition. "The commodity business is the business of risk," said a Rich trader to explain why his boss became the target of the largest tax evasion case in United States history. "Marc can be the prince of fucking darkness. He got caught because he took more risk than any other trader in the world."

CHAPTER 2

"Pay no attention to the man behind the curtain."

THE WIZARD OF OZ to Dorothy
after Toto pulled back the drape
and exposed the wizard's scam.

ONALD REAGAN was dead. The stationary aneurysmatic bubble wedged into the president's middle cerebral artery since birth violently exploded without warning on St. Valentine's Day, 1984. The pressurized mixture of blood and water blew a hole in his brain while he was discussing a solution to the Lebanese crisis with Egyptian President Hosni Mubarak at 11 A.M. EST.

The snippets of the rumor of Reagan's death that had trickled over telephone and telex lines by 4 P.M. GMT hit the London trading houses with the impact of a hollow-point bullet. The story had apparently leaked from a high official on the Securities and Exchange Commission to a yet unidentified New York Commodity Exchange (COMEX) floor trader within minutes of the president's death at 11 A.M. EST. For the next thirty minutes the prices of gold, silver and platinum would bounce higher than a Wham-O super ball. By 4:15 P.M. GMT the price of gold skyrocketed $12 an ounce. The fluctuation made Robbins nervous. He was trying to get his hands on all the gold possible, but nobody was selling. "I'm short gold and in some minor trouble," Robbins confided in an uncharacteristically nervous tone from Unicoal's London office in the shadow of Marylebone Station. "I've been selling gold that I don't have possession of all morning, and the last gold I got my hands on was $5 an ounce more than I'm contracted to sell it for."

Robbins was convinced that President Mubarak had furiously splashed Reagan's face with ice water from a chrome pitcher on the Oval Office desk as the White House physician sprang into the room with a contingent of Secret Service agents pushing an intensive care unit crash cart. The water did not help; herniation was swift. The turgid balloon spumed blood throughout Reagan's skull, and the viscid matter was pushed down into the brain stem with a pulsating force. Before the physician could make it to Reagan's side, the president's body jerked up from behind the desk and quivered like an autumn cornstalk in an Iowa twister before slumping to the floor.

The commodity tactician and master metal trader of the giant raw materials outfit Unicoal was certain of his information. Like dozens of other metal merchants who had heard the death knell in London and New York, Robbins gripped his telephone with a sweaty palm and punched out numbers, trying to scoop up gold, silver and platinum; there was no official confirmation yet from the White House press office, but New York metal traders kept insisting that the presidential corpse was already cold. That was all Robbins needed to know. One report from the floor of COMEX in New York (the largest gold buying and selling supermarket in the world) claimed that the White House physician had lifted Reagan's eyelids to discover a deposit of yeasty shards scattered throughout the optic membrane. Another trader for Shearson Lehman American Express reassured his London colleagues that Vice President George Bush was in the process of being called back from the funeral of Yuri Andropov in Moscow, and that an umbrella of United States fighter planes from Mannheim air base was waiting to provide air cover for Bush's plane once it had penetrated West German airspace. Another broker at

30

Amalgamated Metal Trading in New York verified the AmEx trader's news account and added that the White House had embargoed the report until Bush had made it safely across the Iron Curtain. *Benedicat te Omnipotens Deus* . . . Almighty God bless you.

Robbins straightened up in his chair, opened his eyes wide and ground the butt of a Silk Cut low-tar cigarette in a stained coffee cup carpeted with gray ash. He cast a glance at the other metal traders around the room drumming their knuckles together in anticipation. No one returned his anxious gaze, a silent indication that Robbins was still short gold. He slouched back down into his chair, lit another Silk Cut and tried to formulate a solution to the same problem that confronted his colleague Fred C. Dobbs in *Treasure of the Sierra Madre:* "How can I get some gold right now?"

The Unicoal office was arranged like most trading offices around the world. Desks pushed together to form one large work area, numerous phones convenient to the hand and charts gauging the ebb and flow of metal prices adhering to the four walls. There is very little silence in a trading room. Whatever calm does exist is pierced by the Gatling-gun rattle of the telex machine. A trader's eyes glow like a Maine lighthouse when he hears the bell signifying an incoming message. Some traders go to great pains to customize their telexes like souped-up hot rods. Colorful banners are often hung from the telex's base, making the machine look like a steel soldier carrying the corporate standard into battle. In the world of high trade, to possess a telex is to belong to the fraternity. Those who play the market without benefit of the noisy metal machine are foolish neophytes, traders will explain.

Some 43 million Americans dream of striking it rich by playing some kind of financial market, but less than a thimbleful manage to knock the markets into making major returns on their investments. The metal traders, those men who wrangle vast fortunes in precious, strategic and fuel minerals, demolish markets for profits daily. It is the natural instinct of the metal trader to smash, kick and throttle the competition. And within minutes of Reagan's stroke, a fight for the control of world resources began over jammed telex lines between London and New York. Any fleeting thought these men might harbor for the public good vanished; friendships that existed between them moments before were buried. Sportsmanship is never tolerated. Skirmishes for the control of a commodity often become messy: Lies are elevated to the level of truth. Through it all, small investors—the Carolina farmer and the Seattle schoolteacher—make up the needed armies of pawns. Depending on a trader's position in the metal markets that day, the death of Ronald Reagan was either a macabre way to lose money or a ghoulish plot to reap some quick profits.

Unicoal was a multinational corporation that understood how to knead unstable markets to make big dough. The company was formed in the mid-1970s, when American coal mines were posting profits of 20 cents a ton. A group of slick geologists had banded together eight families who operated nonunion mines in Tennessee, Virginia and West Virginia. The families had been unwittingly digging bituminous coal from the same geological reef, and the geologists knew that the price of that coal could rise if the families worked the market together. The new confederation, Unicoal, pumped up its coal profits nearly $100 a ton, making overnight millionaires out of hardscrabble mining men who still nursed large blue bruises on their foreheads, a brutal by-product of spending too many years bumping their heads against mine ceilings. The small town of Grundy, West Virginia, became Unicoal's world headquarters, transforming a once depressed valley into an Appalachian Beverly Hills.

The good life that Grundy's burghers had grown accustomed to almost disappeared when Jimmy Carter was elected president in 1976. Carter created regulations requiring any coal mining company that sold its product to a federal utility to abide by expensive mining safety standards. Unicoal, a nonunion operation that employed unskilled labor, viewed the guidelines as damaging to their profits and decided to stop selling to federal utilities. Many in the company considered the decision capricious, but it turned out to be a brilliant stroke. Unicoal began flogging American coal to fuel the hungry steel mills and power plants of Germany, England, Japan, France and Spain. And as the oil crisis drew to a close in the United States, the price of domestic coal collapsed with a thud. But Unicoal's profits soared from the sale of its unregulated coal abroad. The Appalachian miners had effectively parlayed laws that would have crippled the company domestically into loopholes that regenerated Unicoal into an internationally powerful outfit of strategic metal traders who used coal cash to bankroll Robbins's metal market speculations.

By 4:15 P.M. GMT Robbins began to believe that a gruesomely clever market hustle was being masterminded by a small clique of COMEX gold traders. There were New York gold traders twisted enough to instigate across-the-board hoaxes, but for one of their lot to declare Reagan dead would be simply criminal. And one thing continued to gnaw at his doubts about Reagan's death being little more than a vile hoax: The story was being confirmed by virtually every trader he spoke to in America, and when a lie is confirmed in the metal business, the savvy trader accepts it as fact. There is always money to be made, even in lies.

"If Reagan is alive then why doesn't he take one of his Hollywood walks out on a White House balcony and wave to some bloody tourists," Robbins moaned to a business associate at the London headquarters of Billiton, the multinational metal-trading arm of Shell Oil. "I heard that some asshole came out of the White House press office around 4:15 and said that he had seen Reagan thirty minutes before and that he looked all right. It sure stinks fish to me, and I'm not going to be caught short by Reagan dying."

Reagan's stroke had finally gutted the tenacious bear gold market. Since February 1983, bullion had taken a disastrous plunge from a high of over $510 an ounce to a low of $365 in January 1984. The petered-out price represented a drop of 28 percent, and the experts said it reflected Reagan's efforts to decelerate the inflation rate, as well as high United States interest rates, a strong dollar, drastic cuts in OPEC oil prices and overly adequate world gold reserves. The economists even had a complex mathematical formula to spell out the process. Economic equations, however, have a nasty habit of falling apart in times of crisis. Theoretically, there should have been enough gold to fill the short positions of dealers who had futures contracts due that day, but not even the average daily turnover of 100,000 ounces on the London gold market was enough to supply the demand. The instantaneous lack of gold came as no surprise to Robbins. "In 8,000 years of gold mining," he said, "we have only managed to recover about 88,000 tons." It wasn't much gold, hardly enough to fill the display cases of cosmetics on the ground floor of Bloomingdale's.

The search for gold had become desperate at 4:25 P.M. GMT. Switzerland's famed banking gnomes, who control the Zurich gold market like a family of trolls, were reluctant to part with any of their horde. Samuel Montague, Johnson Matthey, N. M. Rothschild, Mocatta and Goldsmid and Sharps Pixley—members of London's exclusive club of gold-price fixers—also had no metal for immediate delivery. Gold brokers on the Chicago Mercantile Exchange echoed the sentiments of COMEX. Hong Kong bullion brokers were just going to bed.

The dollar began to post a drop against all major foreign currencies, creating a situation that frazzled metal merchants, for they were committed to converting bushels of American greenbacks into the foreign currencies with which they had contracted to purchase their freighters and warehouses of industrial minerals. Brokers in New York were now reporting that videotapes of Mubarak chatting with a living Reagan in the Oval Office had been released to the networks. But the time of the taping was not released. The omission fueled more fear. Robbins grabbed his phone and began ringing friends at the *Financial Times*, Reuters, the White House newsroom and the brother of someone he once knew who now worked for *Business Week* in Washington. All London calls to COMEX were answered by shaky-voiced floor traders who incessantly reconfirmed that Reagan was absolutely dead and, more important for the moment, that there was no gold to be found outside of what South African Harry Oppenheimer had yet to dig out of Namibia. The question still being asked at 4:27 P.M. GMT by every trader short the yellow nugget was "Can you get me some gold?" The answer continued to ring a hollow "No."

Word spread.

"I heard it on the floor at around 11 A.M.," the voice of AmEx vice president Peter Grote crackled over a transatlantic phone line from lower Manhattan. "Yeah, yeah, I'm telling you it sounds awful possible. I'm sitting here in my office, and it comes over the loudspeaker intercom we have hooked up to our traders over on the COMEX floor. The White House denied the whole thing, but it sparked a rally in gold and silver the likes of which we haven't seen in a long, long time."

"The dollar is going to collapse," hectored the German metal trader in a harshly clipped voice during a hastily arranged conference call with his associates in New York, Düsseldorf and London. "Buy whatever gold and silver you can find to cover our short positions, but get our hands on some long dollars against the mark. If Reagan isn't dead, then we'll make the money back on the cheap dollars."

"Listen, I'm telling you, all the voice said was that Reagan was dead," London commodity broker Nigel Watts bellowed to Robbins. "We have a direct communication link with COMEX, and our chaps tell us the man is *dead*."

The life or death of Ronald Reagan was inconsequential by 4:30 P.M. GMT. The market was precious and strategic metals had gone delirious. Robbins had been in the metal trade for over a decade. He had risen to superstar status by the age of thirty-two because of his canny ability to read and dissect market movements quicker and more accurately than the competition. Robbins had given closed-door intelligence briefings to United States congressmen on world metal stockpiles and had been the confidant of mineral-rich Third World despots. But right now all his years of training and contacts added up to a hill of beans. He knew that no information, no market, could remain fully consistent. By nature, markets involve balancing competing buyers and sellers in a frustrating and explosive world. Inconsistency and a lack of cohesiveness are the cornerstones of the trading fraternity. Robbins understood that this strange economic architecture compelled traders never to do anything halfway, and people who deal in such absolutes are destined to cause trouble, particularly on exchanges where political upheavals further distort already manipulative situations.

And it was trouble that was percolating on the floor of the London Metal Exchange, the small arena in the City of London, where forty pugnacious dealers from the world's major metal brokerage houses pounded out the world prices for silver, lead, zinc, aluminum, tin, copper and nickel. LME brokers buy and sell metal in a series of five-minute trading rings. Haggard men, they slump on soft red leather chairs around a brass plate resembling a cheap tray from the Tangiers souk. Individual brokers bark out what they have to buy or sell, and at what cost, in between the coded gasps, sneezes and screams from assistants who are in constant contact with the trading offices through a bank of phones situated a few feet behind each dealer's seat. Any trader who wants in on the action attempts to out-holler the competition, and if anyone disagrees with which trader the buyer or seller chooses, a referee decides who first opened his mouth. "England outlawed pit bull baiting in 1835 and legalized the LME in 1837," explained a hoarse ringmaster from Johnson Matthey. "On a slow day it's maniacal; on a heavy day you're fortunate to walk off the floor alive."

The acoustics of this tiny pit had become so wretched that the LME board of directors had decided to suspend huge panels of white-painted plywood from the ceiling with industrial-strength chains, the kind used to lash down ships during a full hurricane. The wood was supposed to dampen the noise, but it only ricocheted off the three-inch ply as the brokers fought to buy silver contracts during the market's closing five-minute silver ring, beginning at 4:35 P.M. The pit was jammed with perspiring bodies and strained faces seeking out phone clerks for more possible information on Reagan's death. A phone receiver was accidently ripped from the wall by an overeager assistant trying to relay information to his partner. Ring referees were uselessly pleading with brokers to remain calm. By 4:39 P.M. the brokers' howling pleas for silver ingots sounded like prayers from invalids begging to be cured at Lourdes. It was quickly turning into one of those days when a trader would be lucky to get out alive, let alone be blessed. All the pit lacked was a pendulum.

Doug Lee, the managing director of Intertech Resources, sat behind mounds of blue-tinted telex messages piled atop his desk, looked at the afternoon LME prices and began to snigger at what was taking place on the world metal markets. The editors of the influential trade publication *Metal Bulletin*, the *TV Guide* of the multibillion-dollar metal-trading business, referred to the thirty-five-year-old market whiz as "Dapper Doug" in their biweekly "Hotline" gossip column. Lee's two trademarks were his eclectic tastes in clothing and his unusual ability to turn around failing companies—specifically, the smooth sophistication he used to turn badly beaten metal-trading firms into heavyweight contenders for a piece of the crowded international marketplace. By the time he was twenty-nine years old, Dapper Doug's magic had transformed the floundering metal-trading firm of Derek Raphael from a $35-million-a-year backdoor operation in 1977 into a $200-million-a-year powerhouse with solid trading partners in Eastern European capitals, behind the forbidden walls of Beijing and at the dining tables of the Kremlin. He left Raphael with a fat bonus in 1982 to regenerate the mom-and-pop trading group at Cambridge Metals into the most successful small strategic-metal sales outfit in Europe and America. Now at the helm of his own trading company, Doug Lee was having a good belly laugh at the concentrated weirdness displayed by his metal-trading colleagues.

Dapper Doug's insight and reputation had made him one of the commodity world's most popular sounding boards during marketplace freak shows. Zebby James, Lee's fiery Irish blonde assistant, was assuring panicked traders from around the globe that her boss would be more than happy to take their calls if they could only hold on and lower their voices. After a few minutes of brisk conversations, Lee had persuaded metal men in Germany, Japan, Spain, France, Italy, Switzerland and Hong Kong—and a drunk specialty steel maker in Sweden—that Reagan was most likely alive and that "some bozo" in New York was probably long on silver and wanted to push up the price and get out of the position before going off to lunch at the Four Seasons. "I must tell you that no one wants to believe it's a scam," Lee explained while fondling a Valentine chocolate bar fashioned to resemble a bar of Crédit Suisse gold bullion. "These things happen all the time, and the result is always the same. A few people are going to go home tonight with a great deal of money, and a lot of people are going to visit a bar to drink away all the losses.

"If I'm wrong," Lee added impishly, "you can buy me a double vodka and tonic after the silver ring closes because I won't be able to afford it."

Ronald Reagan rose from the dead at approximately 4:47 P.M. GMT, and Dapper Doug Lee sauntered past the pub on his corner and drove his metallic gray BMW to Harrods. The stroke that felled the president and elevated the closing gold price to $379.75 an ounce, a healthy $2.50 higher than the day before, turned out to be a brilliantly executed scam by a few gold and silver traders in New York, acting under orders issued from high atop a Swiss mountain. The rumor was ignited allegedly to raise the price of silver (which in turn raises the price of gold) because the company was long on silver and the price was falling steadily. Reagan's death bolstered the silver price nearly 20 cents an ounce—a substantial price jump for the metal men, for whom a minimum silver contract constitutes 10,000 troy ounces. And why not? Spinning yarns to exploit unwanted assets has been a cornerstone of the economic system since Rumplestiltskin.

"Whoever started the rumor was very smart," Lee mused, while poking through a wicker basket of loud polka-dot bow ties on the ground floor of Harrods. "If you get more than one personality involved in starting a market rumor, it adds much more credibility to the scam. I must say some of those pit dealers are real professionals at starting rumors. It's a lot of bullshit, mind you, but you can't help admire them in an odd sort of way."

"The imagination and taste of people involved in the commodity markets are at somewhat of a low standard," said a groggy Peter Grote the morning after Reagan returned to the living. "The structure and psychology of the marketplace are not always good. We often do not have the best interests of the public at heart. It is unfortunate that it reaches the level of game playing, but some of us must create these situations, these opportunities, just to get out of positions we should not have been in in the first place."

Although the trickery and turmoil that whipped the metal markets in New York and London on February 14, 1984, sounded as legal as off-loading Bolivian cocaine at the Statue of Liberty, venality carried the day. An investigation official from COMEX responded to the entire, extraordinary deception as if the illusionary death of a United States president were a natural way for individuals and corporations to remove themselves from unwanted financial positions before lunch: "If we investigated every rumor that swept the marketplace for possible illegality," prattled the COMEX solon several days later, "then all COMEX would ever do is investigate rumors."

The price of gold, silver and most strategic metals sky-rocketed that St. Valentine's afternoon, which slammed the dollar back 1.5 cents in thirty minutes. The day after, cupidity soared when those traders who had bought cheap dollars made small fortunes selling them again.

"Even the downing of the Korean airliner didn't do what Reagan's death did this afternoon," babbled a trader for Marc Rich International over double martinis at Morton's, a fashionable club on Berkeley Square where the metal men gather after the market closes. "Shit salesmen, that's what we are. Two hundred people get killed and gold doesn't move. Say that Reagan's dead and we'll make at least two dollars an ounce.

"Who can we kill off tomorrow?" he slurred darkly. More Russian vodka dusted with Italian vermouth primed the dialogue, which was no longer funny; it was an alcoholic black comedy, scripted by a trader scared that forces he could not control would bring a similar manipulated tragedy to one of his own positions the next morning.

PART II
RAGS TO RICHES

CHAPTER 3

As I recall, Marc has the frame to become a pretty good baseball player, but he never owned a mitt.

A FORMER FRIEND

WHEN THOSE PEOPLE who know Marc Rich try to explain what made the man, they all begin with Antwerp, the city of his birth. At first glance, Antwerp is a curiously silent city. A continuous drapery of thin cloud flutters over its pristine streets, the scud falling gently away into the surrounding countryside. The shafts of sunlight, winter and summer, somberly highlight the petroleum refineries, industrial mills, assembly plants, textile factories and Old World farms that shutter Antwerp from the North Sea, fifty-five miles down the deeply dredged Scheldt River.

Antwerp was a town built by cultured men and managed by businessmen. Christophe Plantin, the foremost master printer of the Middle Ages, refined his artistic techniques in Antwerp, printing financial broadsheets for the wealthy merchant class. Masons chiseled the city's panorama into a picture postcard dominated by a 400-foot Gothic spire; they were also commissioned to construct the bourse, Antwerp's sixteenth-century stock exchange. Splashes of bright color, in the form of Rubens masterpieces, inject life into the otherwise dull, modern office blocks. The archaic and guttural-sounding Flemish language is still the preferred language of the corner vegetable sellers, harshly clipped Yiddish the vernacular of the Hassidic diamond arcade, and when pressed, everyone speaks their own peculiar brand of French patois.

Antwerp proffers a cleansed beauty, a flavor too bland for one of the continent's melting pots. The piquancy that enlivens business cities such as New York and London has been scrubbed out of Antwerp, leaving a homogenized life for businessmen, who roam the lunchtime harbor like owls, listening to the grinding purr of anchors being mechanically dragged back aboard ship. But the inscrutable sterility of Antwerp lends itself to the conduct of business. The city is a temple of learning in that respect, an imposing fortress of silence where business can be noiselessly transacted, prudently understood.

Before World War Two, David Reich had come from Frankfurt, Germany, to join the thousands of Antwerp's Jewish merchants, a massive enclave of struggling dealers who were constantly importuning the rich Ashkenazi traders for a slice of the industrial trade they controlled. David Reich was not a wealthy man nor a member of that small band of elegant Jewish businessmen who would flee, impeccably dressed aboard luxury steamers, the sound of invading Nazi jackboots. David Reich was a low-level trader pursuing one of the few occupations offered to Jews: buying and selling anything available that would turn a profit. It was a business born in the back alleys of the Industrial Revolution, in the effluence of factories, where tired and oppressed Jewish merchants pulled junk-laden wooden carts in the hope of making a few coppers by selling scrap or a discarded bolt of soiled cloth.

Jewish traders, many of whom constructed empires from selling their wares off rickety barrows, were known as rag and bone men, the characters who would arrive at the back door or the factory gate to scoop up whatever had been thrown out. In the process the tribe of rough-and-tumble traders developed an international network of buyers and sellers, ultimately making them sought-after middlemen to supply goods such as metals, leather, cloth and gems. But success did not come easy to men like David Reich. Trading was, and remains, a heartless, sometimes vulgar game peppered with heavy-mannered and bare-knuckled business techniques that taught the Jewish merchant how to survive, above all else.

Pelikaanstraat, Antwerp's most famous commercial street, bears witness to the city's deep Jewish trading roots. Hugging close the ancient facades, elderly Orthodox Jews in fur caps and ear locks scurry between buildings with cases and pockets full of diamonds. The business of diamonds, like all businesses in Antwerp, is not showy. The swirling tempest that hallmarks the North American diamond market center on Manhattan's 47th Street would be out of place here. Business in Antwerp is swaddled in silence. Negotiations are conducted in quiet back rooms, behind inviolable doors, and with the utmost of discretion. The lessons of doing business in Antwerp were uncompromising, and David Reich would insist that his son understand their ruthless dynamic. It was into this life that Marc, the only child of David Reich and Paula Wang, was born on the afternoon of December 18, 1934. It appears that Marc spent most of his youth alone, following the lead of his strict parents who had few close friends. It was a childhood of anonymity, shattered only by the domineering presence of his father. The overbearing influence David Reich had on his son was more than an inheritance; it would come to settle over him like an ever present shadow of a statue.

Like thousands of other impoverished Jews fleeing the Nazi nightmare, the Reichs made their way to the United States sometime in the early 1940s, first landing in Philadelphia. With the help of a Jewish placement agency, the family was soon resettled in Missouri and their surname Americanized to Rich. The first glimpse of Marc Rich's life in America appears in 1944, when the Richs moved into a first-floor apartment at 4404 Holly Street in Kansas City. Former neighbors recalled that the family was laconic and entertained few visitors. Marc, who then spoke only French, was enrolled in the E. F. Swinney Elementary School, a typical inner-city school infused with a culture his father would never permit him to understand fully. Rich's parents ruled his life with Old World determination: Marc was their son first, a Belgian Jew second and an American kid last—and only if he had the time. But there was little time. His hair the proper length, his clothes never muddy from the playground, Marc Rich moved on to Westport Junior High School. And although he became a United States citizen on St. Valentine's Day 1947, his life at Southwest High School in 1949–50 was not an endless summer of malt shops, football games and cheerleaders in the back seat of dad's DeSoto.

Marc Rich did, however, become a Boy Scout; thus the summer of 1949 found him at Camp Osceola in the Ozark Mountains. "He kept to himself," remembered Calvin Trillin, a *New Yorker* magazine writer who as a teenage camper lived for two weeks with Rich in the same "chigger-filled" tent. "Skipper Macy ran the camp, and one day after lunch he started off on one of his famous campfire talks. The topic was languages, not one of your normal subjects at Camp Osceola, and he started asking if anyone there could speak more than one language. Rich put his hand up. The Skipper asked if anyone spoke three languages and Rich again put up his hand. Rich just kept raising his hand as everyone looked on in amazement. As I recall, he spoke French and German.

"The funny thing is that Rich was the quietest kid at Camp Osceola, and he's the only fellow camper I remember," Trillin added perplexedly. "There was just something about him."

The student from Antwerp who spoke three languages made no lasting impression on the high school teachers and students of Kansas City. School records indicate that Rich was an "inferior to mediocre" student, participated in no activities and attended few classes. His classmates at Southwest High School, some of whom are pictured near him in the yearbook, have absolutely no recollection of the lanky, bushy-haired kid. "It's hard to believe that a guy could have come through Southwest and have little contact with his classmates," mused Marvin Rich (no relation), who graduated from Southwest in 1952. Marc Rich, by all accounts, lived his high school years in solitude, a teenage ghost.

Rich's father, meanwhile, in 1946 used what little money he had brought from Antwerp to open the Petty Gem Shop, a cheap costume jewelry outlet on Kansas City's East 11th Street. He upgraded the Petty Gem Shop into a wholesale jewelry distribution center in 1948 under the name Rich Merchandising Company and moved his headquarters into the linoleum-floored Sharp Building. "I had no idea who was working in that office," remembered Victor Prudden, an optometrist whose office was located across the hall from David Rich's suite. "That man made no impression on me."

By the late 1940s the family, armed with a $10,000 bank loan, purchased an $18,000 red brick house at 429 East 72nd Street. Long-time residents of East 72nd Street, like everyone else in Kansas City who had any contact with the immigrant family, said that the Richs made no lasting impression. "As far as I am aware," recalled one Jewish woman who lived near the Rich home, "the family never involved itself in the Jewish community." On May 16, 1950, the Richs sold the house and moved to Queens, New York, departing Kansas City as quietly as they had lived there. It was a solid and practical European posture. The family asked no questions and sought no answers from the culture that a distant war had forced them to adopt. For David Rich and his family, Main Street was replaced by Pelikaanstraat the moment the front door was closed.

David Rich had left Missouri with his family to enter into partnership with Bronx businessman Maxie Korngold. Rich and Korngold managed the Melrose Bag and Burlap Company, a trading firm that imported Bengali jute to manufacture burlap bags. The Melrose Bag and Burlap Company, like everything else in David Rich's life, was enveloped in

47

silence. The company never even joined the Bronx Chamber of Commerce, something that the chamber considered "odd" in a community where membership came with the address. Melrose Bag and Burlap was the foundation for David Rich's varied and successful business ventures. Within ten years, profits from Melrose would allow Rich to expand into retail fashion jewelry, spare car parts and tobacco speculation. He made frequent trips to La Paz, where he eventually teamed up with Bolivian businessmen to form Sidec Overseas, a diversified agricultural trading company selling everything from flour to bicycles to sewing machines, to the landlocked Andean nation. In the late 1950s, Rich plowed Sidec's trading profits into a banking venture and started the American Bolivian Bank with his Bolivian business partners. "He was very personable, caring and extremely intelligent," one of Sidec's former employees said. "He started with a small department and jewelry store in Kansas City and became a man of means." David Rich did not agree with the culture swirling around his family in the wealthy American paradise of Queens, where he had installed them, but he became an American millionaire, the embodiment of the immigrant's dream.

At first, however, Marc's future did not seem as bright. Poor grades and a uniform lack of distinction at Forest Hills High School prompted Rich's parents to enroll their son in Manhattan's Rhodes School, the prep school known to New York City as a "rich man's reformatory" from its subway car advertisements proclaiming "Be a Rhodes Scholar." Records from his senior year at Rhodes suggest a bright student, one who did poorly in math but presided over the French club. Observing Rich in a 1952 classroom report, one apparently clairvoyant teacher described the "shy" student who would become the most dominant and commanding trader in modern history as "purposeful, actively creative, strongly controlling, deeply and generally concerned, assuming much responsibility and exceptionally stable."

"Marc Rich took his education extremely seriously," Don

Nickerson, Rhodes's present headmaster, advised. "His record shows a very ambitious young man who under today's standards would be a straight-A student. It's funny though; here's a student who had one hell of a time with math going on to become a millionaire."

The kudos did little to fire Rich's personality or endear him to fellow students. "Marc never had many friends," remembered one of his classmates at Rhodes. "He was always alone, he kept to himself, the kind of kid you'd want to poke fun at." The evaluation of Marc Rich—earnest, conscientious and essentially dull—was not a result of Rhodes training, but an immutable product of being the only child in the household of David Rich. His life was different, punctuated with German, a relentless language of command, the language of the trader. "I always had the impression that no matter how much his father loved him, the relationship was more along the lines of master and apprentice than father and son," explained a New York City jewelry dealer who knew the family. "You could sense the pressure whenever you were around them."

Marc Rich was graduated from Rhodes and, with his father footing the bill, entered into the four-year marketing program at New York University in the fall of 1952. By all accounts the halcyon quality of Greenwich Village in the fifties escaped Rich totally. He had been raised to be a trader because his father had been a trader and his grandfather had been a trader and that was all he knew. New York University bored him quickly. His chance to get out came in early 1954.

Philipp Brothers, the largest raw material trading company in the world, was scouring American universities for young men they could snatch and mold into *lehrlings*—the Yiddish word used to describe young men apprenticing to be traders. The man in charge of the program was Henry Rothschild, who, like everyone else at Philipp Brothers, had escaped the Nazi holocaust.

Rothschild had become a *lehrling* in Cologne, Germany, at the age of ten and had no problem encouraging Rich to sacrifice a college education to become a trader at Philipp Brothers. The company, in fact, preferred to educate their people in-house, the traditional European approach and the Philipp Brothers way of doing business. *Lehrlings* were trained to trade every commodity known to man. The company was run like a large family. Department heads such as Rothschild acted like stern fathers, not executive vice presidents. And in Marc Rich, Rothschild sensed something special.

"Marc wanted to learn the business and he came from a family that understood trading," said Rothschild, who knew David Rich as the salesman who provided burlap bags to sack the company's Bolivian ore. "It was a good hire. Marc had the patience to learn.

"You didn't have to pay *lehrlings* a lot of money. It wasn't like today," Rothschild recalled. "I taught Marc how to make calculations in his head, trained him in the finer points of the metal business and commodity trading. What I taught him was traditional knowledge of the profession."

Marc Rich first entered Philipp Brothers' Pine Street office in the spring of 1954; at the federal courthouse a few blocks to the north, Judge John McGohey was in the process of sentencing crime boss Frank Costello to five years in prison for evading $51,095 in taxes. Walking past the newsstand in the lobby, Rich probably never noticed headline stories describing Costello as a businessman who "spent a lifetime making money on the shady side." There was no need. Marc Rich was about to be trained by a clannish group of German-Jewish traders who held no interest in such matters. It was an ignorance that many of them would live to regret.

CHAPTER 4

When you want something from a person, think first what you can give in return. Let him think that it's he who is coming off best. But all the time make sure that it is you in the end.

SIR ERNEST OPPENHEIMER

THE LOBBY OF THE McGraw-Hill Building is dappled with majestic slabs of brown marble. Loitering is forbidden and crisply uniformed guards will drive along the unwary if they spend too much time poring over the quotes from Plato and John Kennedy on the wall on flattened ingots of bronze. A business address at the McGraw-Hill Building is an impressive pedigree, and the service elevator operator is quick to inform the uninitiated that despite the name of the building it's Philipp Brothers who are the top dog in the Rockefeller Center skyscraper. The awesome scope of the metal and commodity trading conducted on 152,075 square feet of space comprising five entire floors is best seen by glancing at the directory of businesses choreographed from the twenty-fourth floor: Phibro Asia, Phibro Development and Management, Phibro Distributors, Phibro Energy International, Phibro Exploration, Phibro Export Sales, Phibro L.P. Gas, Phibro Mineral Enterprises, Phibro Oil, Phibro Oil and Gas, Phibro Resources, Phibro-Salomon, Philipp Brothers, Philipp Brothers China, Philipp Brothers Commodities, Philipp Brothers Corporation, Philipp Brothers Grain, Philipp

Brothers Holdings, Philipp Brothers Korea, Philipp Brothers Trading Center, Philipp Midwest Metal.

The twenty-fourth floor's corporate roster is the inheritance from an Old World dream shared and nurtured by two hard-working German brothers who began peddling scrap and brokering small deals on the Hamburg Metal Exchange in the 1890s. The brothers Philipp parlayed their contacts in Europe's old-boy Jewish trading network to emerge as one of the major suppliers of metal to European industry during the prosperous years before World War One. Julius Philipp was the front man, an intoxicating broker with the charm to convince nineteenth-century mining companies that he should sell their ore once it left the Earth. Oscar "Opie" Philipp was the desk jockey, a short and rotund whip-song dealer who it is said could sell metal back to the mine his brother bought it from, and at a profit.

Philipp Brothers was a family operation that could just as easily have been run out of a kitchen as it was from an office. And as the company expanded, Oscar and Julius ensured that it remained that way. When they opened their first foreign office in London in 1908, it was cousin Siegfried Bendheim who was sent to pave the way for dealing on the London Metal Exchange and selling mineral additives directly to Britain's booming steel industry. Oscar followed a few years later and became outraged immediately over the height of the people he had to do business with in his new environment. Not a trader to be outdone on any of life's commodities, Oscar dispatched his London *lehrlings* to find and bargain for the largest desk in the British Empire from which he could rule his empire with equal stature.

What Oscar lacked in height, however, was more than made up for with the cunning resourcefulness he used to keep the German metal-trading firm alive in Britain during World War One. Britain had a law requiring that all corporate letterheads list the nationalities of directors at the bottom of the page, and Oscar knew that the disclosure would destroy the efforts of Philipp Brothers to establish itself as a trading power in Britain. Oscar once again turned to his apprentice traders, calling upon them to scour the libraries and bring back any scrap of information that he could use to hedge the fact that Philipp Brothers was a German firm. Cousin Siegfried's Germanic roots had already forced him to avoid being interred in a British detention camp by escaping to America where, of course, Oscar told him to set up Philipp Brothers Trading New York.

A glitch in the law was found quickly. It turned out that if a business in Britain was over 100 years old, it did not need to list the nationalities of its directors on the letterhead. Oscar unearthed Britain's corporate rolls and found a small eighteenth-century brimstone company called Derby. He purchased Derby for a song and made the company the new owner of Philipp Brothers in the United Kingdom. Like the huge wooden desk that is still in the London office as a monument to the elfin might of Oscar Philipp, Derby remains one of the operating names for Philipp Brothers in England.

But the most important decision that would ever be made at Philipp Brothers took place an ocean away, inside the Woolworth Building during the final days of the American Depression. It was in those grim hours before the outbreak of World War Two that Siegfried Ullmann, who followed Bendheim to America to run the brothers' New World operation, sent a cable telling distant cousin Ludwig Jesselson in Berlin to catch the next boat to New York City. Jesselson was twenty-seven years old, a hot product of Aaron Hirsch and Son, a century-old metal-trading firm where he first cut his gums as a *lehrlings* messenger at the age of sixteen.

Ludwig Jesselson's life made him the Everyman candidate for the American dream. His father was a poor farmer and a part-time rag and bone man from a small village a few miles beyond the smokestacks of Heidelberg. The future that Philipp Brothers could offer first caught his attention while he was still a trader for Hirsch in Hamburg and Amsterdam during the depths of the Great Depression. And Philipp Brothers was

53

well aware of the talents of Ludwig Jesselson. By the time Jesselson was twenty-five years old, he was a trading genius, one of those rare men with a talent to coalesce ingenuity and determination into every deal he made. He calculated the most difficult of figures without the aid of a pencil, rolled off the mineral requirements of obscure factories with unsettling accuracy, directed company assets into new trading ventures with the alacrity of a field marshal deploying troops and developed the deepest of heartfelt friendships with everyone he touched. Ludwig Jesselson had the fiber to become a one-man trading machine, and Philipp Brothers wanted him in their powerhouse.

Jesselson had acquired an American visa in 1927, but the American consulate in Berlin told him that it would be better to sit tight until the Depression was over. At the time it was difficult for Jews to get the necessary documents to come to America, and Jesselson sensed that the Depression was just an excuse to make matters more difficult. But the persistence (often pigheaded) that he would soon use to help reconstruct Philipp Brothers was turned on the American consul. He virtually lived at the consulate, cajoling, reminding and charming. Jesselson received the necessary papers. When Ullmann finally offered him an office in the Woolworth Building, Jesselson caught the first boat to New York City.

The American system of free enterprise pollinated the trading genius of Ludwig Jesselson. Along with Ullmann, Jesselson seized the mandate to foster the presence of Philipp Brothers on the industrial scene and sculpted the company into an omnipresent trading force throughout the world. When Jesselson started to crank up Philipp Brothers in America, the company's foreign presence was limited to small excursions to deal for metals in Canada and Bolivia. But within fifteen years he would spin an international web of producers and consumers dependent upon Philipp Brothers to serve as their middleman in times of feast and famine. "We thought nothing of working twenty hours a day," Jesselson said. "I knew how to make money, but that never meant anything to me. It was the people and the trust and friendships we shared. If I made a deal, I honored it like the Holy Bible, even if it meant losing money."

The strength Ullmann and Jesselson brought to Philipp Brothers was the ability to mold solid long-term contracts with dozens of international metal producers. Their game plan was to purchase the rights to a mine before the first rock was out and then handle every aspect of the physical movement—shipping, warehousing, insuring and sampling. The credo was simple: Philipp Brothers would always deliver. This gave the company the singular advantage of promising industry a continuous supply of raw materials far beyond their own current needs, allowing them to plan for the future with greater financial accuracy. The metal contracts Jesselson made permitted cost-conscious manufacturers to sleep easy because Philipp Brothers always delivered material at the price originally agreed upon, even if the free-market spot price had skyrocketed at the time of delivery. But the flip side of such nimble transactions was a customer paying more if the spot price dropped well below what he was contracted to purchase it for from Philipp Brothers. Ullmann had an almost foolproof gambit for those instances when customers would trundle into his office to hector about variations in price. Sitting behind his desk like a kind priest taking confession, Ullmann would at first sympathize with his customer's financial plight, a posture guaranteed to catch the visitor off guard. When the upset buyer was done complaining, Ullmann's character changed to one of kingly detachment. He produced a massive gold pocket watch from his vest, snapped it open with a firm click and stared blankly into the crystal.

"Do I get the impression that you want to cancel?" Ullman roared, his eyes glued to the pocket watch and no more sympathetic than those of a wounded lion.

Buyers became unnerved. On cue they would begin to mutter a rambling answer. Ullmann cut them off immediately.

"I'll give you one minute to decide," he commanded, his eyes not budging from the watch. "If you want to cancel, it must be now."

The customer, now totally uncertain where his best interests lay, never weaseled out of the deal, deciding it safer to pay the higher agreed-upon price than to return to his office to find the spot price twice as much as it was before he encouraged the wrath of Ullmann, a man who would throw fits if he discovered an upside-down postage stamp on a Philipp Brothers letter. "Genius," Jesselson said of Ullmann, "is very fragile." Ullmann was tough and fear-inspiring, but he also had a motherlode share of Philipp Brothers compassion: In the mid-thirties a trader needed a few thousand dollars to make ends meet and took an unauthorized cash advance. Ullmann found out about it and tore into the trader like a buzz saw. Calming down a bit, Ullmann finally inquired why the trader didn't come to him for the money. The trader shook his head back and forth. Ullmann took out his personal checkbook and asked the trader how much he needed, no questions asked. Whatever side of the trade a dealer was on, life at Philipp Brothers was a long-term contract not easily broken.

Philipp Brothers' compacts with the miners in South America, Africa and Asia also captivated the banks, who saw the company's alliance with producers as the perfect collateral for issuing large loans and astronomic letters of credit. Jesselson and his traders traveled the world like silent diplomats, using their gold-plated portfolios as potent weapons in convincing the Third World that it would be good business to be allied with Philipp Brothers. Not only would Philipp Brothers offer the best price for their material, they told the mineral producers, but if their mine ran into financial or political difficulty, Philipp Brothers would be there to help bail them out. It was, of course, good business. But to Jesselson and the German-Jewish traders at Philipp Brothers, it was a heartfelt extension of the family ideals taught by their fathers. Old World Jews such as Jesselson knew painfully well that trading was once

the only game offered the Jews and that it stemmed from the
dislocation and poverty of the Jewish community. The family
had kept them together through the rough times, and it was
natural for Jesselson to use those same hardscrabble values to
ensure that they would never again be forced to push rag and
bone barrows like common tramps.

Nowhere did the company's kitchen-table style of business
prove itself better than Bolivia, where Philipp Brothers remains the major conduit for the troubled Andean nation's
outpouring of tin, tungsten and antimony. The association
between Philipp Brothers and Bolivia began in 1927, when
Arturo Gruenebaum opened the company's first La Paz office,
and has transcended the 356 assorted coups, elections, military
upheavals and states of emergency that have rocked the country ever since. One of the men who went there was Henry
Rothschild, whom Philipp Brothers had lured away from Associated Metals in 1946. By the time Rothschild had arrived
at Philipp Brothers, Jesselson had become the firm's top trade
negotiator. Rothschild, who would eventually run the trading
arm of Philipp Brothers alongside Jesselson, quickly assumed
the role of troubleshooter. "I got the fireworks and Jes lit the
fuse," Rothschild says. "We were the perfect team." Rothschild was no simple high-road executive who traveled the
world just to negotiate for minerals. He was the personification
of the Philipp Brothers trader. Rothschild crawled down into
Bolivian mines, picked away at veins of tungsten ore alongside
coca leaf–chewing miners and had the bejesus scared out of
him on more than one occasion when the decomposed corpses
of 500-year-old Indian miners fell out of ancient underground
holes and buried him in pitch black tunnels 300 feet beneath
the Altiplano. Such feats, however, were part of the job description for all Philipp Brothers traders.

But it was back in the conference rooms at La Paz where
Jesselson's trading teams really polished themselves in the
compulsory exercises of international business, which others
found so difficult to shine in. Philipp Brothers became a trad-

57

ing behemoth because they applied the theory that money advanced on purchase of metal will be returned long before money advanced on paper. The whole international banking system is predicated on a leap of faith that Philipp Brothers never accepted. The banks continued lending, and the borrowing nations kept repaying the interest so that, although the principal might be rolled over for individual nations, the money remained in circulation. But as a United States Senate report on international banking pointed out, "The biggest threat to the system lies in the possibility that one of the passengers on this merry-go-round will decide to get off—that one of the larger debtors finally decides to repudiate its debt, or one of the lenders says 'no more' and calls in the chits." Bankers, Rothschild said, never questioned the promises of sovereign nations to repay their debts. Philipp Brothers did.

"The banks never knew what they were doing lending money to the Third World," Rothschild said, citing the $98 billion Brazil, $93 billion Mexico, $35 billion Venezuela and $45 billion Argentina currently owe American banks. "Even back then we understood that these countries were heading for trouble. We lent Bolivia money, still do. But their collateral is their mineral wealth, something that there is always a market for. If the bankers had gone into these countries like traders and dealt instead of just give, give, give, then you wouldn't have all these nations lining up to default and blackmailing the banks into giving them more. We've been telling the bankers this for years, and they never listen because their situation is motivated by politics."

"Philipp Brothers always tried to never be political," Jesselson said. "We look at developing nations as if they were bicycle makers. Bicycle makers are just not equipped to market bicycles, so they go to someone else to take that risk. Philipp Brothers exists to assume a producer's risk. To accomplish this a trader must be a worldly man. He must be versatile and able to trade for anything. He must be honest and open and love to deal. It has always been my belief that

58

international traders can do more than anyone else to foster peace, friendship and stable economics among nations."

Philipp Brothers thrived and grew rich off the crises that disrupted trade during the Second World War. Ullmann and Jesselson created trading commando units to crack neutral states such as Spain and Portugal and outbid the German Reich for strategic metals needed for the American war effort. "I spent three days flying to Brazil on a DC-3 in 1942," Jesselson said. "Our man in Rio and I went into the jungle with some natives carrying hand shovels. All I remember is the diarrhea." Two months later Jesselson emerged from the jungle with critical loads of Amazonian minerals needed to manufacture military smoke bombs.

The clandestine trading teams worked closely with the Office of Strategic Services throughout the war. "Whenever we saw Germans buying some metal, we bought even more," Jesselson recalled. During the height of the war, Jesselson found himself in Portugal, where his network told him the Germans were about to purchase an ore he was not familiar with. It didn't matter, Jesselson reasoned. If the Germans wanted the ore, it must be important. Jesselson outbid the Nazi traders and snatched away a shipload of uranium ore-bearing rocks that were warehoused and later given to the Atomic Energy Commission.

One of the company's boldest search-and-acquire missions took place in the old Belgian Congo (now Zaire), where Philipp Brothers traders out wheeled and dealed the Nazis for caches of tantalum, cobalt and columbium necessary for bullets, bombs and warplanes. German intelligence alerted Wolf Pack commanders and ordered them to torpedo the Philipp Brothers convoys as they crossed the South Atlantic. But Philipp Brothers—who always delivered—did something that no one had ever done before. They quietly arranged to fly container ship–sized loads of metal back to America under the cover of night. Winning the war was also a personal battle for the Philipp Brothers family. A few days after Nazi bombers

59

leveled Rotterdam, the Amsterdam office was gutted by the SS. Julius Philipp was driven away in a cattle truck to be murdered for being a Jew.

Traders at Philipp Brothers always had to move faster than the speed of sound. Jesselson instructed his people to change their mind about a price or a delivery the moment they got an inkling that some unseen market force (or a U-boat) was afoot. But getting solid information quickly was difficult. Before the advent of computers and telex machines, the price of a metal was established whenever the mail arrived and stayed firm for about three months. Jesselson encouraged the use of telegrams for everything from up-to-the-minute prices to the strength of Third World regimes. He developed a series of traffic codes for each metal and its price, a system that was designed to save money on telegraph bills and not to conceal prices, as is done today. By VE Day the amount of information filtering through Philipp Brothers trading rooms had propelled the company from a small group of German-Jewish traders who, as Jesselson said, "only got into the business because trading metals was the only business opened to us" into the commodity world's most irresistible force, in a perfect position to establish the ruthlessly pragmatic trading patterns for the Nuclear Age.

The first thing Philipp Brothers did was strengthen the ties they had established with America's allies and the Third World during the war. Jesselson made scores of trips abroad, and in 1948 found himself on the Orient Express bound for Yugoslavia for "no particular reason." On the exact day he arrived in Belgrade, Marshal Tito broke all ties with the Soviet Union, an event that Jesselson knew would leave Yugoslavia's rich reserves of copper, silver, lead, bismuth and antimony up for grabs. Without contacting New York, Jesselson went in and cut a long-term deal that made Philipp Brothers the sole broker for Yugoslavian mines. "Doing business with the Communists in 1948 was like making a deal with Dracula," Jesselson said of his enterprise. The New York office found out about the deal along with the rest of the world days later when it was reported over the radio.

While Jesselson made deals, Rothschild was dispatched to open the first of what would become fifty full-time foreign offices sending news of commodity developments to New York at a rate of one message every twenty seconds. Rothschild structured the Philipp Brothers outposts in Thailand, India, Peru and Brazil, and set the standards for the ones that would follow. Jesselson wanted on-the-spot Philipp Brothers traders wherever the company had an interest. The use of agents was strictly forbidden because Philipp Brothers would have no quality control over the purchase or shipment of a material. "You can't rely on agents," Jesselson told his staff. "Agents are not interested in Philipp Brothers. Agents are only interested in making their commissions."

The traders Philipp Brothers hired to fill these posts in the early fifties were handsomely developed and exceptionally coordinated by Ullmann, Jesselson and Rothschild. Traders in Europe were under the direction of Dr. Adolpho Blum at Derby, which by 1950 had changed its corporate structure to become a partnership between Oscar Philipp, Nathan Issacs, Henry Levy and Philipp Brothers. Derby had already established a foreign foothold in the Commonwealth nations, and the new guard being hired in America would ensure that it remained firmly in place.

Entrepreneurship and eagerness were encouraged. Traders were trained to always ask, "What can I do to improve a market situation?" If the ego of a Philipp Brothers trader was bruised by the cyclical downturn of a fickle market, Jesselson would intervene to soothe the wounds like a father consoling a son who skinned his knee sliding into home plate. And if a trader got in trouble, Philipp Brothers was always there to take care of the problem. The stories of Jesselson helping his traders with money or time off have assumed the stature of coffee-break legend at Philipp Brothers. If a trader's child was ill or his mortgage payment late, it was Jesselson who quietly took

care of matters, believing it to be no more than his duty as
head of the Philipp Brothers American household. Gratitude
was, of course, expected, but fierce loyalty to Philipp Brothers
was demanded. "It was a holdover from the old days," Ben
Bollag, who spent thirty years at Philipp Brothers, explained.
"Both Ullmann and Jes honestly believed that there was no
need to pay traders lots of money because Philipp Brothers
would always be there to take care of them."

"Jes" Jesselson, however, had one tragic flaw: He never
knew how to muzzle the aggressive nature of his young traders. "Jes never lost a nickel on a trade, but he lost people by
pitting them against each other in the office," said Hubert
Hutton, a former Philipp Brothers trader and friend of Jesselson's. "He often overvalued aggressiveness."

CHAPTER 5

There is a universal tacit agreement among all traders to take from each other increase for their products, to work in the dark in their dealings, to play a sharp game; in a word to take each other by surprise by all the tricks of the trade.

PIERRE PROUDHON,
Nineteenth-century French economist

LUDWIG JESSELSON is a nostalgic monument to a time when the business of business was less acute and the relationships between men were glued together with trust, not corporate lawyers. Philipp Brothers was a firm without need of Golden Parachutes, leveraged buy-outs, secret agendas, Mary Cunninghams. Jesselson was always there to support his family, cultivate them in the trading techniques they would need to lead the next generation of Philipp Brothers traders. There were no executive recruitment firms employed to spend millions in finding people worthy of leading Philipp Brothers into the future; *lehrlings* like Marc Rich were tomorrow's leaders, trained in-house, and Jesselson considered the idea of looking elsewhere to be the bitterest of humiliations. Trading was an arcane and unpredictable game that Jesselson, like a sorcerer, made predictable for the apprentices who came to Philipp Brothers to trade the Earth's crust between nation and industry. It was a philosophy that demanded total and immediate candor between Jesselson and his *lehrlings*.

Trading called for a quick and facile mind, and while other

corporate executives aggrandized themselves to get ahead, Philipp Brothers traders just didn't have the time to partake of such superficial corporate fashions. The Philipp Brothers' totem was a hierarchy of shrewd deals, not inflated vanities; getting to the top demanded a talent to tame the furious chemistries of volatile markets. And Jesselson gladly taught these men how to balance these tensions. He showed them that it was possible to remain humble while retaining the ability to endure.

The first thing Philipp Brothers did before hiring a trader was to administer a simple test to see if the prospect possessed a talent for calculating figures. Jesselson believed that a trader should be able to calculate in his head or with the occasional aid of a pencil. (To this day Ludwig Jesselson has never used an electronic calculator. Years ago he was given one. It still remains in its original box, held together with rubber bands, in the bottom drawer of his desk.) If the prospective *lehrling* displayed a capacity for figures, he was hired and placed in the traffic department, where he would learn how to ship material around the world under the guidance of Sam Fishman, the master mover of Philipp Brothers.

The ethos of the trading mentality hinges on nerve and, when in action, like a soldier, being able to control fear. The traffic department of a trading organization is the best place to teach the control of fear because it is the closest thing to war. If a trading passage was closed to ships with Philipp Brothers' material on board, then it was up to the traffic manager to discover the alternative route. Such problems forced traders to be inventive and to realize when to be daring. There was no room for fear or disenchantment, because the material had to hurdle whatever obstacles had been placed in the way. Young traders admired Fishman, impressed with his ability to blank out fear as an inferior form of nerve. And Fishman was the action man on whom all trades hinged. It did little good if a deal was concluded and the material never made it to the buyer. It was up to Fishman and his young trainees to fulfill the Philipp Brothers promise of always delivering.

The traders who entered Fishman's classroom were varied in nature, background and style. David Tendler, the man who would start in traffic at $75 a week in 1960 and end up as chairman of the board with a salary in the millions, was a hard-nosed kid from New York's Lower East Side who got excited looking at maps and traded bananas during summer breaks from City College of New York. Many of the traders hired by Derby out of London never "did traffic." Alan Flacks, a university dropout who started at £70 a week in 1954, was thrown immediately into the deep end and sent to India within days of his being hired. "When we started there were guys here our age who had been trading since they were sixteen years old," Tendler said. "These guys came up from the mail room, had no college education and were more experienced than all of us put together."

One of the traders who entered Philipp Brothers' New York traffic department in 1954 was Marc Rich, the "tall man with the soft voice and the strained smile who always wore Saks Fifth Avenue suits."

"He was not the kind of fellow you'd ask out to lunch," said a European trader who sat across from Rich in the early days of his career. "Marc always felt he was brighter than us, that his shit didn't smell. And he never talked about anything except business."

There were about 100 people at Philipp Brothers' New York office and the bureaus in the process of being buttressed in Buenos Aires, São Paulo, Tokyo, Osaka, Ankara, Amsterdam and Zug. It was a perfect time for the $60-a-week *lehrling* to learn the mysteries of moving fleets of container ships between nations, the nuances of complicated bills of lading, the subtleties of figuring out which shippers could be trusted to deliver material intact. Jesselson and Ullman played good guy, bad guy, respectively. Ullman hovered over the young traders like a storm cloud ready to explode. "Ullman scared the living daylights out of me," Tendler said, his eyes flashing back to the fears and insecurities of a *lehrling*. Jesselson stroked and encouraged, using his warm smile as a beacon the traders could follow to realizing the full extent of their capabilities.

"Jes identified with all the young traders, but more with Rich because their family backgrounds were so similar," a Philipp Brothers senior executive explained. "But there was something about Rich that the rest of us never liked. He was always shifty and never engendered trust. He made everyone feel that they always had to be on guard when he was around."

"Rich could be a bundle of sincerity if he wanted to," said a Philipp Brothers trader who worked alongside Rich for ten years. "He was so damn changeable."

Rich's contemporary colleagues found him "aloof, frosty, occasionally irrational, dangerously irritable." But they were double-edged traits that if applied correctly could fine-tune the combat psychology necessary to create a good trader. "Marc's great strength from the day he came here was his incredible impudence," a Philipp Brothers executive admitted coldly. "The man never hesitated to ask for anything; the kind of person you'd throw out the front door and he'd go around and crawl back in through an open window like a sneak."

Bill Spier, a Philipp Brothers trader who would later serve as an usher at Marc Rich's wedding, suggested that Rich's drive isolated everyone at the company. "We were both aggressive hustlers," Spier said. "Marc was always successful and dynamic. We'd come into the office together on Saturdays and read all the weekend mail, find out what was going on while everyone else was at home. What separated our friendship was his belief that you could only make it bigger and better than the next guy by buying people off. Marc was suave and sophisticated and obsessed with power. He was always looking to see who he could buy off."

Rich's obsession with business even carried into his personal life. He still lived with his family and when he did make the time to visit with friends, the get-togethers were all business. He was a frequent visitor to the Fire Island, New York, home of Ralph Meyer, a Philipp Brothers senior executive who became his father confessor. Rich and Meyer would go on ski trips together, but even those were cut short by the ever present telephone calls that usually pulled Rich off the slopes for hours. And when Rich decided that he wanted out of the traffic department, it was Meyer who helped pave the way. "All Marc ever did during his off hours was sit and brood about business," a former friend said. "I spent many weekends with him, and all he ever talked about was business and when he could start making deals on his own."

Rich was Philipp Brothers' fastest learner, according to Hubert Hutton, who had the opportunity to watch Rich grow into a trader. "He had the best memory of anyone at the company and the nature of a true gambler. He never stumbled into anything in his life. Every risk he took was calculated."

Philipp Brothers traders recall that Rich's first big deal was in mercury, the quicksilver liquid leftover of cinnabar broiled in a Herreshoff Roaster. Mercury is one of geology's two-faced creations: It's so toxic that it causes birth defects, but it remains a not-to-be-duplicated ingredient for dental fillings and catalytic converters. Mercury, which has been used since Roman times, first established itself as an industrial mineral in seventeenth-century Europe when felt-hat makers refined "water silver" by treating cinnabar ore with a ghastly solution of vinegar and urine. The mercury was then boiled and the fumes used to stabilize wool. The inhaled vapors, however, caused erethism, a nervous disorder highlighted by irritability and weird personality changes, the so-called Mad Hatter Syndrome. Mercury's price was just as schizophrenic, jumping anywhere between $120 and $800 for a 76-pound cast-iron flask.

When Rich began to trade mercury in the late fifties, the stuff was used for mirrors, thermometers, a cure for syphilis and as a major propellant for the machinery of war. By the Second World War mercury had replaced magnesium in batteries providing more power and making the liquid metal much in demand. Quicksilver was also used in making ammo caps and painted on battleship hulls to prevent the growth of barnacles. The Korean War had proved the "mercury equation," a bit of razzle-dazzle arithmetic that statistically showed the price of mercury always increasing 20 percent the moment a major military conflict ignited. So when the post-Korea war machine began bargain shopping, it was natural that it would call upon Philipp Brothers to fill its orders. Rich found himself dealing the right metal at the right time. He purchased mercury from the Almaden Cinnabar Refinery in Spain and from Soviet quicksilver capitalists and then sold the flasks to various manufacturing plants in America and the Far East. The amount of profit made from Rich's mercury deals has been forgotten, but the creation of the deal was enough to curry the interest of Jesselson.

"It doesn't matter what the commodity is," Tendler said, downplaying the role of luck a trader might have in creating a profitable trading situation in any of the 160 commodities traded at Philipp Brothers. "It's more important that a trader know what the manufacturing role of a commodity is at the precise moment it's being traded."

Marc Rich's sweeping success with mercury resulted from his embracing the market, studying the needs of the industries shopping there that particular day and then getting in an offer. Rich "made a market," as traders say, because he knew that manufacturers needed mercury. He had seized an opportunity and had turned it into a profitable trading situation for Philipp Brothers because Jesselson gave his *lehrling* traders the leeway to explore. "There is no mathematical formula for evaluating risk," Alan Flacks advised. "You have to figure it out on your own."

Jesselson, as David Tendler says, "allowed us to have our own heads." And if a trader made a few dollars on a metal that everyone else ignored, then Jesselson grew excited. "I started playing with zinc dust," Tendler recounted. "It saw an extremely small return, just a little over $100,000. I thought nothing of it until Jesselson heard about it and came running into my office and told me to take off for Belgium on the next plane to talk to the producers. The same thing happened with a fertilizer deal I did back then with South Africa.

"He shaped our growth, let us assume responsibility from a very early age. He knew that we grew excited about the deals and that we would report back to him for guidance and information. And then you sat there and listened to him as if you were attending a lecture."

Jesselson also whisked his traders around the world and introduced them to the buyers, sellers and cultures in which Philipp Brothers conducted business. Nothing, it seemed, was too good for a Philipp Brothers trader. "He really took us everywhere with him," Flacks said. "I remember one of our first meetings in the finest hotel in Zug. Jesselson sat me down for a wonderful meal and wanted to know everything about me and my ideas. He made everyone in the firm feel wanted and genuinely important to the success of Philipp Brothers."

Nineteen-sixty was a watershed year for Philipp Brothers traders, a time when the company supplemented their trading education by making them part and parcel of what at the time was one of America's largest corporate mergers. By the turn of the decade, Jesselson became acquainted with André Meyer, the merger magician from Lazard Frères. Philipp Brothers was regularly posting profits of $6 million a year on a business worth $200 million, but Jesselson knew that the net worth of Philipp Brothers could be dramatically increased if the company went public and that Meyer was the man to make it happen. Under Meyer's direction, Philipp Brothers merged with Minerals & Chemicals Corporation, an already publicly owned company that made kaolin, a petroleum-cracking catalyst that helped break down heavyweight oil into plastics and gasoline. Minerals & Chemicals Philipp Corporation was born in July 1960 and sent a lightning bolt immediately across the international trading landscape. Jesselson and Ullmann, the two top principals of the merger, were now worth over $20 million and in a position to restructure Philipp Brothers for the future.

"The merger was done to safeguard the firm," Jesselson insisted. "There were a bunch of old men running the place, and it would have been detrimental if they passed away without a solid structure to keep Philipp Brothers alive."

The public offering made Philipp Brothers the new darling of Wall Street, and Marc Rich became the in-house wunderkind who cooked deals in his head while tooling around Manhattan in a red MG-TD roadster. Impressing Jesselson with the slick style he used to close deals in metals ranging from arsenic to tungsten, Rich was the trader Jesselson could always count on to "make a market." But Rich became more than one of the men dubbed to lead Philipp Brothers into the future. "Jes considered Marc to be his son," a Philipp Brothers director said. "Marc always used that to his advantage."

Rich also played the intimate dinner parties Jesselson gave the traders at his Riverdale home. He would arrive at the door with the most expensive of gifts, a Tiffany crystal bowl here, the latest Polaroid camera there. "He always brought the most fantastic gifts," a former Philipp Brothers trader said. "Even then, Rich was different from the others."

"This is going to sound like bad blood," a trader who knew Rich said in a chilly voice, "but all of us knew that Rich was truckling up to Jes whenever the opportunity presented itself. You just knew Rich was setting him up for something. Why Jes never sensed it, I don't know."

Back in the office, Jesselson constantly referred to Rich as a son, the trader to whom he would impart all the secrets, all the knowledge necessary to carry the Philipp Brothers banner to glory in the second Industrial Revolution. "Jes's kids never gave him any *nachas*," a friend explained, using the Yiddish word for "joy." "Marc gave him *nachas* and Jes saw him as the kind of man he wished his own sons could be."

Rich, decided Jesselson in 1958, would be sent abroad to continue his education and develop his contacts at the company's global outposts. The first stop was Havana, where Philipp Brothers needed a troubleshooter to go in and assist Ramon Villegas and Ernest Frank in dealing with the collapse of the Batista government and the new regime of Fidel Castro. "Marc cut his teeth in Havana, and the experience shaped his character because it taught him that being illegal was okay under certain conditions," said a former traffic manager who dealt with Rich while he was in Havana.

Cuba had been a theme park for bribery and payoff under Batista, and little would change during the opening days of the Castro Revolution. Most of the Cuban metal deals involved copper concentrate, maganese ore and nickel, and were conducted across the bars of the El Presidente and the Nacional hotels. Traders swarmed Cuba, arriving with portable typewriters on which they drew up and signed contracts on the spot. "It was the Paris of the Western Hemisphere," a metal trader who did business in Cuba remembered. "We all thought it would be more of the same with Castro in charge. By March of 1959 we were all eating our words."

Havana's streets were sweltering with revolution when Rich landed, and Castro's cadres were directing their heat at American businesses friendly to Batista. Rich spent the latter part of 1958 and most of 1959 shuttling between New York and Havana and worked the docks, filling the pockets of ship captains to get Philipp Brothers' nickel and copper out of the country. Chase Manhattan was the big American bank in Havana, and Rich was a frequent visitor. "Money always had a way of solving problems in Cuba," the traffic manager said. "It was the way to do business in Cuba. Rich was told to get our material out any way he could. In that situation it was necessary."

Cuba was an environment totally removed from anything Marc Rich had ever experienced, and it smacked of just the kind of exploitation necessary to conduct business in the Third World. "Cuba was Marc's first taste of the illegal," a friend of Rich said. "He saw the potential." The mystique of Ha-

71

vana, an infatuating blend of opulent corruption and romantic revolution, was a fertile business opportunity for traders who understood that money clips were more important than passports when it came to crossing borders.

"Marc always saw Cuba as a place where the rules didn't apply and he came back to New York with what he learned," Bill Spier said.

Jesselson's next assignment for Rich was La Paz, the site of Philipp Brothers' first foreign office. Rich traveled South America and made the occasional hop across the Atlantic to Amsterdam and Madrid. And no one was happier than Ludwig Jesselson when Marc Rich came back to America to marry Denise Joy Eisenberg in Temple Emanuel in Worcester, Massachusetts, on October 30, 1966. It was the perfect match for the future head of the Philipp Brothers household. Denise was ten years younger than Marc, a striking, dark-haired woman whose family had also fled Europe to escape the Nazis in 1941. Denise's father, Emil Eisenberg, was the prosperous chairman of Desco Incorporated, one of the largest shoe manufacturers in America. Their wedding appeared more of a merger than a marriage. The couple had been introduced by their parents, and Rich's ushers were all Philipp Brothers traders. The best man was a cousin of the bride and not a close friend of Rich. "The wedding was like a Philipp Brothers board meeting," a trader who attended the ceremony said. "Everybody talked business." Jesselson, however, was extremely pleased. Marc and Denise, he commanded, would travel the world for Philipp Brothers as a double act.

As the Marc Rich show hit the road, Philipp Brothers was about to close on a deal that would finally secure the dream that Oscar and Julius Philipp shared nearly a century before. Jesselson, through Meyer, merged Minerals & Chemicals Philipp Corporation with Engelhard Industries, the world's largest refiner and fabricator of precious metals. Charlie Engelhard was the inspiration for Ian Fleming's Goldfinger and, more important to Philipp Brothers, was in a position to continue nudging open the door for Philipp Brothers to middle-man the mineral wealth of South Africa through his corporate connections with Anglo-American, the company owned by Harry Oppenheimer.

"The merger was made to create a little romance on the stock market," Jesselson said modestly of the deal. But what happened was more like a gang bang. The new company was named Engelhard Minerals & Chemicals, with Anglo-American as a substantial 22 percent shareholder. Although Jesselson would say that Anglo-American was "just a shareholder like anyone else," the merger allowed Philipp Brothers to slam-dunk South African metal into any world market. Oppenheimer, through his mines, controlled 25 percent of the non-Communist world's gold. His companies also mined rich veins of platinum, vanadium, uranium, coal and nonferrous metals. Added altogether Oppenheimer accounted for almost half of the total of South Africa's exports and half the value of shares traded on the Johannesburg Stock Exchange.

Through a Bermuda post office box holding company called MINORCO, Anglo-American was able to move its money out of South Africa and become the largest foreign investor in the United States, with an estimated $800 million worth of investments in Appalachian coal, Arizona copper, Iowa fertilizer, California gold and Wall Street investment banking through Salomon Brothers. In 1979, for example, MINORCO relied on Engelhard Minerals & Chemicals for some three-quarters of its income. The revenues of Engelhard Minerals & Chemicals posted the score: They grew from $1.4 billion in 1967 to $10.2 billion a decade later. And 90 percent of that money was churned out by Ludwig Jesselson's *lehrlings*, trading, trading, trading.

It was into this burgeoning corporate empire that Marc Rich, then thirty-three years old, was privately designated dauphin to Ludwig Jesselson. The possibilities whirled through his mind like a billion spinning tops.

CHAPTER 6

"Money is your best tool. Men love money more than country, wife, mistress, perversion, reputation, or in some cases, life itself. We can always find clean money to do dirty work. But a warning: He who handles and disburses such money often develops the delusion that it belongs to him. This statement can be broadened, as follows: Power sometimes fills purses, often empties heads."

JOHN HERSEY, *The Conspiracy*

"SECRETIVE" is the one word that everybody uses to describe Marc Rich. Bellhops to brokers all agree that Rich was harder to twist open than a frozen doorknob. "Marc gave paranoia a bad name," a trader who worked alongside him at Philipp Brothers said. "This was not a man who used urinals." Traditionally, a trader likes to share his thrill of victory/agony of defeat hellbroth with fellow dealers because the highs and lows of bucking big odds are surprisingly similar mandatory emotions that need to be shared, unless a trader wishes to toy with being sucked into insanity. That Rich could operate on such an amazingly intense level without any "pals" to go out and get razzled with was an incredible feat.

"There are maybe three people in the world who know Marc Rich intimately," heckled Felix Posen, the pompous manager of Rich's London operation and a major shareholder in Rich's global trading companies. "All three people know different things."

Ludwig Jesselson, however, thought he knew everything about Marc Rich and accepted his nature as a simple quirk because, as a Philipp Brothers director said, "he was a member of the family." But Rich's fellow traders saw him cutting a different cloth. Even Pinky Green, the Philipp Brothers trader who would become the closest thing Rich ever had to a sidekick, told friends that "Marc plays his cards too close to the vest, and it will someday get him into trouble." Rich was aware, of course, that trading was a profession cemented together with silence. If a competitor discovered the inside story of a deal Philipp Brothers was delicately piecing together, then he could effectively use the information to steal the deal away from Philipp Brothers. But Rich had overcranked into a parody of paranoia the idea that the more attention you get the more vulnerable you become. Philipp Brothers executives recounted stories of Rich storming out of informal meetings between traders if they asked a question about or offered to help out one of his deals. David Tendler, the former chief executive officer, recalled one afternoon in 1961 when Rich phoned him in the traffic department, hollering about a problem he was having with an ore shipment. "I had just arrived in traffic and I had no idea what this guy was yelling about," he said. "I didn't need this guy's shit, but I checked and nobody in traffic had any idea what Rich was on about."

Rich insisted upon fast answers and frequently ripped into underlings with savage sarcasm if they were not furnished immediately. That he often neglected to tell subordinates what was going on did not enter into his anger. Rich knew that the reputation of an individual trader was more important to him in the long run than the company he worked for. And those who worked under him were not going to methodically peel away his power by being made privy to deals linking copper producers in Chile to copper refiners in Colorado. No matter where in the world a Philipp Brothers office was located, Rich—sporting a wide and colorful necktie—would rush in before 7 A.M. with a pallor of fear over his dour and sleepless face. "Marc was always scared that someone might have outdone him while he was home in bed," a trader said.

His work pace was relentless and he did not possess a sense of humor. On those rare occasions when he did find something funny, his laugh was one of a man gagging on ill-flavored water. His life was trading, a low-margin, high-volume existence that was only dependent on his capacity to swallow the risk necessary to conduct business in a dozen countries simultaneously.

"A good trader needs imagination and an analytical mind," said Ben Bollag, a metal man who worked the world commodity markets with Rich at Philipp Brothers. "Rich was the undisputed protégé of Jesselson, and Jesselson knew that Rich's genius was his great imagination. Marc's almost childlike imagination was his consummate genius."

Rich's imagination was fueled by Jesselson, particularly in the construction of the huge bank lines traders need to assume risk. Many top traders like Bollag and Rothschild believe that the ability to trade material is a natural talent people are born with, much in the same way a seven-foot-tall Irishman would make a good center for Notre Dame. But traders and basketball players alike must learn to shoot, and to score thirty points a game in trading, you have to be able to deal with the banks.

There is no love lost between bankers and traders, and they consider their unique relationship to one another to be little more than a lusty marriage of financial convenience. Bankers do like that traders need to borrow lots of money to leverage their deals, but a bank will usually not lend a trader money unless he wants to borrow at least $5 million. The big American commodity banks, Chase Manhattan and Manufacturers Hanover Trust, borrow the money they lend traders at around 8 percent interest. Then after a lunch of rare steak and double Jacks, they lend it to the trader at 11 percent interest. The gross profit to the bank on this $5 million transaction is $550,000 a year. The bank then pays $400,000 to their own lender, leaving the bank a tidy sum of $150,000.

The banks leverage lending cash between two and five

times the amount of money a company is worth. This line of credit allows traders to make deals with invisible money, on which, if they do not use it, they are still charged a basic fee by the bank. The credit commission revolves around one-half of 1 percent. When Marc Rich started trading metal, he would usually work a credit line in the $50 million neighborhood, providing at least $250,000 a year to the bank even if he failed to tap the cash pipeline. Since worldwide trades are conducted in a multitude of currencies and not solely American green-backs, the trader will also establish credit lines with foreign banks. He must be constantly wary to avoid any material losses due to fluctuation in foreign exchange rates and hedge any substantial currency imbalances. This legerdemain is done on the hope that the money, other than the fee he pays to the bank for the service, stays invisible. And that is dependent on the metal man taking a profit from the deal he has used the evanescent cash to construct. If he fails to close the deal, the bank coughs up the cash, a figure that could be in the hundreds of millions of dollars.

Over the years Jesselson had skillfully accelerated the relationship between the banks and Philipp Brothers so that by the time of the Engelhard merger the bankers were lined up in the lobby like satyrs waiting to get in on an orgy. Jesselson taught Rich how to tame the banks, pull their interest rates down a quarter of a percent on one deal if they wanted to increase their interest a tenth of a percent on bankrolling another deal with their money. Henry Rothschild, who concocted virtually every letter of credit Philipp Brothers ever signed, because "bankers don't know how to write letters of credit," coached Rich in the wiles of beating the bankers at their own game. "Letters of credit were another trading situation," Rothschild would say. "Someday the bankers will learn how to write them."

Jesselson painstakingly endowed Rich with the ken to use the letters of credit as a magic carpet to soar above the differences between the governments of nations. South Africa,

Russia, China, the geopolitics mattered little to Marc Rich because he had been trained to cope deftly with wars and revolutions. Rich was always the buyer and the seller and, in the process, became a kind of insurance man for droughts, floods and coups d'état. At the office he was haunting and brooding, but there was no one more incomparably sweet than Marc Rich when it came to dealing with a customer. The alfresco lunches he threw for European clients were bigger and better than the competition's, the Christmas gifts he sent to his Italian clients were only outdone by the treasure chests of hard-to-get Western goods he wooed Soviet magnesium producers with at the New Year. Jesselson insisted that Philipp Brothers never offer a bribe to secure supply, but traders who knew Rich during his days abroad state privately that it was Rich, more than any other Philipp Brothers trader, who stretched the fine line between graft and gift. "We heard stories, always stories," a Philipp Brothers trader said, not wanting to believe rumors decorated with wisps of truth. "There was no way to really know, this business moves too fast to operate under total scrutiny. If he did go beyond the limits, I'm sure Jes never knew. Philipp Brothers extending bribes would have killed him." Rich's grand handling of Malaysian tin magnates and Iranian chrome kings, however, kept Jesselson happy because his cardinal rule of dealing was to always treat the customer right.

The trading community admired Rich because he was able to dismantle the sticky web of mercantile regulations and restrictions that hobble the wealth of nations and their corporations. Like the old junk dealers who left no garbage heap unturned in their search for discarded lead batteries, zinc cathodes or copper pipes, Rich explored and took quiet advantage of every opportunity that would add to his power, influence and prosperity. "Rich had a photographic mind," said Cees Van Den Hout, a Dutch trader who knew Rich. "He never made any noise, he looked, listened and remembered." Rich traded alone and silent, a process no individual or government could contain. Life was a series of deals and situations to take risks on. Although nobody at Philipp Brothers other than Jesselson liked his style, he was a force to be reckoned with because he delivered. Rich knew that Philipp Brothers was his vehicle and also understood that it was his steam that made it move.

"The problem with trading is that success breeds the ability to reach out for more and more," a Philipp Brothers director said of the trading power the company bestowed on Rich at a very early age. "Marc's attitude was do anything and worry about it later. Jes was the only one who could stop him." Jesselson, however, never shackled his princeling. On those rare occasions when he did intervene, it was paternal scolding, like a father telling his overeager adolescent that it's a 15-yard penalty for clipping and not to do it again. Jesselson assumed that Rich, having been chastised, would never foul again. Such lessons were Jesselson's way of teaching scruples to his hot-blooded traders. But unknown to Jesselson, Rich had the blood of a rogue.

Although trading became the absolute for Marc Rich, it evolved slowly, unsuspectedly, like a dormant genetic trait that only time can percolate to the surface. To some the profession was a balls-out plunge through mayhem for money; to others it was a nine-to-five grind that put the kids through college and bought the condo in Miami Beach. But Rich was part of a small group of elite traders trained to perceive the business as a higher level of consciousness and Philipp Brothers as their private temple. The stakes were high, often sharp, and produced a mental state heavily tempered with trouble and worry; there was no real serenity, no Zen tranquility when deals turned sour and cash ran short. "The trading world is very fragile," Jesselson would remind his dauphin. "Lots of gossip always going around, so it's better to keep our business close to our chest. That's why our customers rely on us." To survive it was necessary for Rich to handle life like an open auction. Traders described the intensity of a deal in temperature; Philipp Brothers executives often said that Rich's deals were "hot" and spoke of him as if he were cursed by trading: He had to deal, had to transact, constantly, inexorably. On a good trading day—one when a customer wants to purchase material a trader has an ample supply of and at a high price—Rich's eyes sparkled like a kid swapping baseball cards with friends on the back porch. When times were bad, Rich slunk into the gloom of a boy who just lost two Mickey Mantles flipping for one Roberto Clemente.

Rich was a budding genius when he became manager of the Philipp Brothers office in Madrid in 1967. Although Philipp Brothers overseas managers were known as the "lost sons," the Madrid posting was Rich's reward for the years he spent buccaneering between North and South America, Africa and Europe. Rich was now an expert in areas that others only heard about over after-work cocktails. Copper was king at the time, and Rich was one of the metal's crown princes. He had clambered down into Chile's El Teniente, the most productive underground copper mine in the world, making sure that Philipp Brothers got a piece of the 1.3 million metric tons of copper refined from its 1,000 miles of tunnels. He crossed the Atacama Desert to Chuquicamata, an enormous open-pit copper mine, where he talked production with the American managers. He went on to learn tungsten under the direction of Henry Rothschild and Steven Dale, a former British commando who was the tungsten expert for Derby. "If you want to become a trader, then learning the business from a tungsten expert is a great way to get started," a London metal dealer explained. "Tungsten is so strategic that it's used in every type of armament from a bullet to a tank, and it's the only item openly brokered between Russia and China. The power, the politics, the money is all there in that little piece of rock."

Rich had a lot of youthful energy and talent he could have imparted to his colleagues in the Madrid office, but the first thing he did was antagonize everybody there. The European economy was bubbling at the time, and Rich wanted to ensure that Jesselson and the Philipp Brothers board knew that it was Marc Rich who was stirring the brew. Alone. Rich used Madrid as a base, traveling through West Africa and the Mideast, trying to add his two cents to every Philipp Brothers deal in the area. The position of office manager and his seat on the company's European management committee gave him the singular advantage of observing all trades conducted in the European theater and a direct line into the Philipp Brothers European nerve center in Zug, Switzerland. "He'd study the deals we'd make and figure how to use the information to set up his own side action," a Philipp Brothers trader familiar with Rich said angrily.

Since Rich did not possess a valid driver's license, he would usually walk to the office at #18 Fortury. Madrid weather seemed never to bother him; he would canter through the greasy smoke of winter and drizzling smog of summer like a bay gelding rushing to the track for a big race. When he walked with others, the talk was always small; his eyes stared straight ahead, pinched with intensity. Although only in his thirties, Rich appeared elderly, his prematurely thinning hair flapping like twine in the wind, squamous facial lines as though slit by a knife. Rich was oblivious to the *calles* and cathouses of Franco's Madrid, and if he was curious about the riots or sordid details of the streets, he never discussed them with anyone at the office. A London trader in Madrid during those years recalled seeing Rich walking out of the office one gray winter afternoon. "Rich was alone, and a beggar approached him," the trader said. "He gave him a few pesetas. It surprised me because it was not a gesture from the Marc Rich I knew."

"He was so damned cold," a Philipp Brothers trader remembered. "He'd walk into a room and people froze. You knew he was always on the lookout to score points with New York, and if someone fucked up, he'd crawl up walls." It was during this time that Rich began to drink heavily. He drank only Scotch; the preferred brand was Johnnie Walker Red splashed over a few ice cubes. He constantly attended three-course business lunches and threw dinners that were more like Roman banquets. Weight became a serious problem; Rich battled his bulge with capsules of easily obtained Spanish amphetamines washed down with more Red Johnnie. "He was not a drunk," said a trader who worked with him and described his drinking as a "social anesthetic." "He likes to eat and drink. Food and liquor relaxed him, and the speed put him on edge."

Rich wanted to score big and knew that Jesselson considered Madrid the litmus test. If he could overcome the ferocious job tension and make a lasting imprint on the Philipp Brothers high command, then it was a ninety-minute Iberia flight to the position of European manager in Zug and then eventually Jesselson's job as head of the Philipp Brothers traders. Engelhard Minerals & Chemicals was the company name on paper only. The merger had sliced the business into three corporate divisions: Engelhard Industries, Minerals & Chemicals, and Philipp Brothers. Each division was controlled by its own slate of presidents, executive vice presidents, group vice presidents, regular vice presidents and comptrollers. Although Jesselson was chairman and president of the Philipp Brothers division, titles had historically counted for little in any corporate structure involving Philipp Brothers, a fact evidenced in corporate photographs, which never failed to depict Jesselson center stage with the management of each division. There were around fifty-three men running Philipp Brothers at the time, and it was the traders who held all the cards. Since both Engelhard Industries and Minerals & Chemicals needed Philipp Brothers to supply them with the metals and chemicals used in manufacturing, Jesselson's power in this structure was virtually papal: His people scrounged the material, and he called the shots. But by 1969 the relative corporate calm of the manufacturing industry slowly began to shatter around Philipp Brothers.

"Everything started to fall apart when all the manufacturing plants developed by the major industrial nations in the mid to late sixties started to come on line," explained David Tendler. "All of a sudden there was no consumption and you had these expensive factories sitting there doing nothing. There was too much material and no place for it to go."

Matters worsened when the dollar was cut free from gold in 1971. Philipp Brothers was rich and famous because it was the biggest metals and commodities buyer and seller on Earth; it had become so in part because, until 1971, a buyer always knew how much of his own currency he would eventually need when he first bought material using dollars. Floating dollar prices, however, created a maelstrom for both buyers and sellers, causing clients to slip out of their contracts with alarming frequency when dollar prices became too expensive for alien money. "It became increasingly difficult for anybody to continue saying that their word was their bond under those circumstances," Tendler said morosely.

Philipp Brothers had the financial gear to successfully weather dollar breakdowns and limited industrial capacity, but then all hell broke loose in December 1973. It was in that month that the Organization of Petroleum Exporting Countries (OPEC) was formed, a group whose smallest hiccup engendered panic throughout the entire industrial community. It was a trader's worst nightmare: too many goods, no one to buy them. Even if a buyer did show up, the cost would seesaw because of oil price increases and unstable currency markets. But it was a chaos tailor-made for Rich, who, no matter what the circumstances, was always prepared to take that one step beyond. "Marc had a blind spot to what was permissible at Philipp Brothers," a corporate director said. "The industrial slowdown that started in the late sixties and early seventies was a situation he could really run with."

Particularly if he ran with oil.

Jesselson's traders had never been in oil, and the company thought it was a business best left to the oil companies. But early on the young traders were viewing oil through a different lens; they saw it as a commodity and figured it was smart business to trade black gold outside the structures created by the Seven Oil Sisters (Exxon, Gulf, Texaco, Mobil, Standard Oil of California, British Petroleum and Royal Dutch Shell) and the nations who were planning to become OPEC. In 1969 Philipp Brothers unwittingly created the so-called spot oil market—a place where anyone could go to purchase oil without having to deal with oil companies and oil sheiks—when Milan office manager Alan Flacks found himself on the Tunis waterfront. The Philipp Brothers contact in Tunisia had fallen upon 25,000 tons of Iranian crude up for sale and informed Flacks thereof. "It looked like any other commodity," Flacks said. "I found a refiner in Spain who needed oil, then went out and bought the Iranian crude. It was a back-to-back deal, very safe because there was no storage involved and the money was right up front." Jesselson liked the $65,000 profit and encouraged his traders to slowly create oil situations whenever they spotted similar opportunities.

Marc Rich was also concerning himself with oil. Around the same time that Flacks was concluding the company's first oil swap, Rich became chummy with the Iranian chrome dealers whose metal—destined to become, among other things, automobile bumpers—he sold. One of these men was Ali Rezai, an Iranian landowner who walked unannounced into the Philipp Brothers New York office in 1955 holding a lump of chrome ore in his hand. "He demanded to see Jesselson," said a Philipp Brothers trader. "So Jesselson comes out, Rezai puts the chrome in his hand and asks for $10,000 to develop his mines. Rezai sat around New York for two days waiting to get the money."

Rezai returned to Iran with the money and developed some of the country's richest and most productive mines. He became a powerful broker of Iranian intrigues through his friendship with Shah Mohammad Reza Pahlavi and would be "elected" to a senatorial seat in the Iranian *Majlis*. It was through Rezai that Rich developed intimate associations with a number of highly placed Persian ministers and businessmen,

84

among them, members of the Pahlavi family. The Iranian royal family controlled all of the country's oil; a trader who worked at Philipp Brothers at the time claims that Rich, by virtue of privileged information he was receiving from the Pahlavi family, knew that a new oil structure was in the works. "I think that's what first made him leap into oil," the trader confided.

With these few murky grains of knowledge, Rich sowed a deal with the Iranian National Oil Company and began brokering Iranian crude oil to Spain. The insider information and the outsider contact set the stage for Rich's purchasing cargoes of Middle Eastern and later West African heavyweight for hungry Spanish refineries. The moving of oil, however, was a lot different from ferrying container ships of rocks around the world. Oil transport is much more complex and expensive than moving metal and constitutes the difference between fun and trouble for a trader of Rich's caliber. There were new worries like leakage, evaporation and finding the right kind of vessel. They were problems that could be solved only by a master mover, someone who knew shipping like Joe Namath knew passing. Although Flacks got involved in the early deals, the two men never really got along, prompting Rich to find someone more of his mold. He found that man in Pinky Green, the salt-and-pepper-haired Philipp Brothers trader that everybody called "The Admiral."

At first glance Pincus ("Call me Pinky") Green was not the kind of guy you'd nickname The Admiral. Green, a Brooklyn Jew who lived kosher even when he was the Philipp Brothers man in Istanbul, prided himself on being able to transform wherever he was stationed into a little bit of Flatbush. "If you want to find kosher salami in Saudi Arabia, go ask Pinky," traders who worked with Green in Zug would say. Although Green could always fly first class, he opted for coach, standby if possible, reasoning cheerfully: "Why pay more? It's the same plane." His friendly smile became his trademark at Philipp Brothers offices around the world.

"You had to watch Pinky," a former Philipp Brothers traffic manager warned. "He was real nasty behind that smile. If you disagreed with him on a deal, he would call Jes and try to ruin you. Pinky always sold material he didn't have and had no idea where to find. His risk was always too high. You'd tell Jes and he'd never believe you because Pinky was one of the fair-haired boys who could never do anything wrong."

Nothing ever flustered Pinky Green. The story goes that his wife was ready to deliver the couple's first child on a Saturday, the Jewish Sabbath, a day when Orthodox Jews are forbidden to ride in cars. Green helped her into a taxi and shooed the driver to the hospital, where he would follow on foot. "Pinky would not get into that car with her," a friend said. "So he walks two miles to the hospital like nothing is happening and misses the birth of his first child."

Pinky Green didn't miss much else. Clicking like a computer, his mind has instant recall of freight rates, financing costs and shipping routes, talents that he used to make money by swapping identical cargoes on the high seas, pulling down his profit from a difference of a few cents in a charter price. A Philipp Brothers director boasted that The Admiral could tell you where any container ship was at any given moment without first consulting the daily *Lloyd's Registry*. "He was by far the smartest trader in all of Philipp Brothers," Flacks said.

Green was also a seasoned hatchet man who relished disciplining those who he felt had done him wrong. Friends claim Green's professional character was sculpted by an event that took place in Texas while Green was in the service. Green had refused a work detail on the Sabbath and a redneck officer had him thrown into the guardhouse. The post chaplain arrived to get Green out, but the officer in charge refused to release him and evidently began shouting anti-Semitic remarks. Green had to stay in the guardhouse for days until a Jesuit priest managed to get the chaplain general's office at the Pentagon to intervene on his behalf. It was a sad and ugly story that left its imprint on Green's life. "He always told the story, and it made him angry," said a friend. "The event made Pinky more urbane. He saw what the world was really like and he began to respond in kind."

Together Rich and Green were the original Philipp Brothers odd couple and they wrote the rule book for dealing in spot oil, a crazy-quilt trading business built on leverage, depreciation, cash flow and pure spleen. When the first tanker of "Marc and Pinky" oil left Iran for Spain in 1968, the oil trading industry as it is known today did not exist. Oil-rich countries like Saudi Arabia, Nigeria and Iran sold their entire supplies to one of the Seven Sisters, who in turn traded the oil among themselves and a few independent outfits. Rich knew as early as 1967 that over 60 percent of the Western world's processed crude was locked into British Petroleum, Exxon, Mobil, Gulf, Royal Dutch Shell, Standard Oil of California and Texaco. The remaining 40 percent was also controlled by the Sisters and their client nations but processed by others.

During the twenty years before the Arab–Israeli War of 1973, oil prices and production levels were determined by the Sisters, but as the Arab countries and later OPEC upped the ante in the oil pot, pressure to change the system caused a problem. Led by Iran, the other oil nations badgered the major oil companies into increasing oil output to generate higher revenues at the pump in spite of the world market being supplied adequately. Rich, who had been trading for the mineral wealth of oil-producing nations at the time and was privy to insider information, knew that this glut would lead eventually to an oil apocalypse of sorts and that a smart trader could create a profitable situation from the ashes.

CHAPTER 7

Not being always able to follow orders exactly, nor attain to the excellence of those he imitates, a prudent man should always follow in the path trodden by great men and imitate those who are most excellent, so that if he does not attain to their greatness, at any rate he will get some tinge of it.

NICCOLÒ MACHIAVELLI

THERE WERE PEOPLE who at the time thought Rich mad; the idea of an oil being traced on-spot or as a futures commodity was considered extraordinary, if not bizarre, especially since there was so much oil around. "The oil companies were still awash with cash at the time," a Philipp Brothers oil observer explained. "During the fifties and sixties the oil companies were paying out about 15 cents per barrel and realizing $1 per barrel." But when OPEC expropriated the oil production facilities controlled by the majors, the Sisters found themselves to be deficit suppliers; that is, they did not have enough oil to meet demand. By 1972 the seven majors shared some 82 percent of OPEC oil exports, a percentage that would continue to drop as OPEC established government-to-government deals with individual countries as well as with independent traders selling large quantities of oil to small refining firms outside the majors' sphere of influence. The demand for oil remained high, and Rich, having Philipp Brothers' unlimited bankroll behind him, was in a position to fulfill that demand at whatever price the market would bear.

Although the oil-producing nations were more than happy to increase their bank accounts by unloading their supplies to Rich, the fabulous size of the cargoes bowled over Philipp Brothers. The average crude tankers hauled anywhere between 30 million and 100 million gallons of oil, and if the trader didn't have someone to purchase it, then Philipp Brothers was left to pay the storage, insurance and freight. "Oil prices have always moved more slowly than metals and Philipp Brothers was used to seeing fluxing markets," said a trader who has dealt oil for Rich and Green. "Philipp Brothers knew that to make real profit they'd have to trade huge quantities of oil and to do that they had to assume financial risk virtually impossible to hedge on."

Using Philipp Brothers' bank lines, Rich and Green embarked on oil deals without informing New York of the details. There were no hard and fast rules to trading oil, so they made them up as they went along. The oil deals were framed the same as metal deals: They would purchase oil from the producer and then sell it to a refinery, presumably at a profit. Jesselson looked upon the new venture as yet another breakthrough for Philipp Brothers, particularly since Rich's first deals were back to back: Any oil that he purchased was already lined up with a buyer, thus avoiding costly storage and any potential drop from the purchase price. But Jesselson was responsible to the board of directors, and they were none too pleased with the risk Rich was assuming on their behalf. The company's annual reports during the late sixties and early seventies, in fact, neglected to even mention Philipp Brothers' involvement in oil trading. The 1974 report's letter to shareholders told of net earnings of $110,164,000, some 110 percent ahead of the previous year. The percentage of profits was ascribed to fertilizers, ores, precious metals, mining, refining and marketing. Oil profits, which totaled in the millions, however, remained conspicuous by their absence. "The board was scared at the time. The oil business was too crazy and so tightly controlled by OPEC and the majors that many felt our positions could be wiped out overnight," a Philipp Brothers trader explained. "The company was willing to speculate on commodities because we knew what we were doing. With oil we were the new kid on the block."

Jesselson's faith in Rich and the potential of the new business at first won out over the grumbles of the Minerals & Chemicals board, who were, after all, not traders. Jesselson reasoned that if Philipp Brothers traded oil with the same judiciousness it applied to trading other commodities, the only losses would be posted by the competition. But oil was never a commodity that could be traded under a controlled situation, and many at Minerals & Chemicals were wondering privately if the oil companies would react to the new business in the same way Minerals & Chemicals would respond to an oil company becoming involved in trading metals against Philipp Brothers. Jesselson won all the early skirmishes, an executive said, because "he saw Rich making another market and let him go with it." The oil deals pleased the other young traders, but Jesselson and the Minerals & Chemicals management were still stone-cold terrified. And in the spring of 1973 Rich used his authority as Madrid manager to conclude an oil deal that thinned the blood of New York board members. Rich contracted to scoop up large tracts of Iranian crude at $5 a barrel over the current spot price. The board finally freaked out. Not only had Rich committed some $150 million of Philipp Brothers' money to a commodity not one of them understood, but he had purchased the oil above the spot price without first lining up a buyer. For businessmen trained to maximize the use of every dollar spent, the deal had the enervating unreality of science fiction commerce. "Management gagged," a Philipp Brothers trader said. "Here was a trader in Madrid not one of them really knew betting the mortgage on a price rise in oil."

The executives in New York were filled with fear and foreboding, dead sure that Rich was positioned to wreak more havoc on Philipp Brothers than Sherman let loose on Atlanta. According to Philipp Brothers insiders, Jesselson phoned Rich in Madrid, nudging, cajoling and finally ordering him to find a buyer and sell out before the market came tumbling down. Rich told Jesselson that the New York brass didn't know what they were burbling about; the price of oil, he assured Jesselson, was going to zoom. "Philipp Brothers was a public corporation," an executive there at the time said. "If the stockholders knew what Rich was up to, the board would have been hung out to dry." The pressure from New York forced Rich reluctantly to find a buyer and get out of the position at a small profit. The head office's timidity angered Rich and the other Philipp Brothers oil traders. Rich, who had become their leader in this daring new venture, had been rebuked sharply and was apparently shaken by the move, viewing it as an unwarranted tirade against his talent and sanity. The more he thought about it, the madder he got. He had planned to store the oil until the end of the year because he sensed that unseen market forces were about to blow the oil business apart. Rich had told his doubters that the Arabs would probably embargo oil in the autumn, but nobody believed him. When the Arabs did embargo oil that October, causing the spot price to explode to $13 a barrel, nobody in New York called to say he was right.

"Oil scared the pants off Jesselson at first," said Bill Spier, the former Philipp Brothers trader. "The money was just too big for him to handle. Jesselson always walked the office worrying that the oil deals were going to blow up in his face."

Rich was still doing tens of millions of dollars in safe back-to-back oil trades for Philipp Brothers, remaining the firm's leading crude dealer. But no matter how many petrodollars gushed from his deals, Jesselson never let him enter the petroleum twilight zone—the intense upper level of trading—because oil was a business essentially controlled by forces that the company could never hope to contain. Rich—forever looking for fresh bait—decided that one of the best ways to lower the risk in dealing oil alongside the Sisters and OPEC was to go out and buy Philipp Brothers an oil tanker.

Green thought financing an oil tanker to be an excellent idea full of tax advantages and one that would make it much easier for him to move oil from country to refinery with one less middleman to pay. In November 1973 the pair made a verbal agreement to purchase a Greek oil tanker, but the board got wind of it before they were about to close and again asked Jesselson to intervene. It was one thing for a Philipp Brothers trader to go back and renegotiate an already existing contract or clarify a deal closed with a handshake, but when Rich returned to the tanker seller, he did something that many Philipp Brothers officials now believe may have been a first in the history of the company: He welched on a deal.

The message was clear. "The world changed in 1973," Jesselson said matter-of-factly. "The old ways of trust were gone. Everybody started breaking contracts. Prices were changing too quickly for people to keep their word. The value system I had built the business on changed. Trading has never been the same since then. Everybody got greedy." The rugged individualism that Jesselson nurtured in his traders was being drastically curtailed when it came to oil because of the new economic backdrop. Profits in oil were nonetheless enormous and would eventually amount to a third to a half of the company's trading revenue. But the early deals were back-to-back deals for the most part, and anything beyond that scope was considered too risky. Rich's oil deal profits for 1973 alone were estimated in the $5 million range, a staggering sum for a trader who was relatively new to the game and who had to deal with having his hands slapped constantly by the board. Despite such gains, the "hot breath" of a public corporation was beginning to restrict the versatility and ingenuity a trader like Rich could call upon when dealing oil. And Rich, who thrived on the day-to-day hazards of big gamble trades, was badly stung by a bunch of well-behaved and faceless New

York executives unable to accustom themselves to the peculiar craft of the modern-day trader. Other than Jesselson, who was also under new restraints, these men could never understand how far the gap was between managing and trading. None of them, Rich honestly believed, could ever comprehend the monumental chutzpah required to cut a deal. Rich was the brittle-eyed, cold-blooded supertrader who had successfully navigated Philipp Brothers into the unexplored waters of oil trading. He knew the leaks, charted the angles and never grew exhausted or unraveled by the fear that limited lesser businessmen. His attitude was one of trench warfare: Fix bayonets and charge. Rich's feelings were sincere and strong: If Philipp Brothers intended methodically to veto his deals, forcing hasty abandonment of his well-plotted money-making schemes in favor of less exhilarating trading routines, then Marc Rich was going to weave his own web. But he could not timidly leave the company for a job at another trading house. No, he wanted to climb heights that Jesselson would not attempt even in his dreams. Yet one problem still gnawed at Rich: How could he handle Jesselson with enough flourish to come out on top? Rich needed to make a big noise, create some kind of grand triumph and hideous horror that Philipp Brothers and Jesselson would never forget. He soon hit upon a way.

It was a time-honored tradition for Philipp Brothers traders to go and haggle for their yearly performance bonuses with Jesselson. Although Jesselson was a generous man, he turned into a Dickensian Scrooge when it came to actually paying his staff. Who the trader was mattered little; salaries were grudgingly doled out like allowances, and when it came time to negotiate bonuses or ask for raises, traders walked into Jesselson's office like frightened children. When David Tendler was transferred to Japan with his entire family in tow in 1968, Jesselson authorized a mere $33,000-a-year salary, including bonuses and living expenses. "I could have used more," Tendler recalled dazedly. "I didn't have the guts to ask." The traders emerged from these meetings bleach-faced and blurred, scampering back to their offices to lick their wounds, vowing to leave Philipp Brothers like children fantasizing running away from home.

Alan Flacks, now chairman of Philipp Brothers, thought it might be clever to approach Jesselson for a raise while they were outside the office and in the Milan airport in 1965. "I was making around $18,000 a year," Flacks, who was then in charge of the Milan office, recounted. "I wanted, no, I needed, $20,000 a year to make ends meet.

"We were in the waiting area to catch a plane and I thought the time was finally right to ask. I will always remember exactly what he said to me. 'Alan, you're asking for a mammoth increase.' He knew what I was going to ask before I asked."

Jesselson's tight fists infuriated Rich, who had always talked about branching out on his own under the protection of a private corporation that would not be responsible to stockholders or government scrutiny. "From the time we were thirty-three years old it was really all we talked about," Bill Spier recalled. "It was our dream because we'd be on our own making more money than Jesselson would ever pay us. Jesselson never once gave us an equitable bonus, no matter how much money you made for the company."

Jesselson did this to remind his traders that he was still the chief monger even if the Philipps Brothers household was being managed by an inflation-conscious board of directors. And no matter what the circumstances, Jesselson scented when he was about to be hit on. He possessed a canny ability to tool up without notice. Jaw set, palms pressed firmly down on his desk, Jesselson turned frosty and objective whenever the subject turned to salary or bonus. And if a trader began begging for more—a frequent occurrence—Jesselson would first stare impenetrably, then scowl with the ferocity of an old crocodile being taunted.

Philipp Brothers traders, who were being paid anywhere from $85,000 to $100,000 a year including bonuses by the early seventies, departed from these meetings feeling more like liveried servants than high-strutting international businessmen, their egos lying smashed and strewn around the office like Styrofoam coffee cups. Rich had long ago lost interest in wriggling through the yearly danse macabre with Jesselson. The smarmy "Son of Jesselson" routines, coupled with what Rich perceived to be the conservative bent of the New York board, had by the end of 1973 set the stage for his dramatic departure. Rich was a wilding, the one Philipp Brothers trader everybody could count on to bear a ruthless grudge longer than a Hell's Angel. "Rich saw Jesselson constantly second-guessing him," a trader said, trying to explain the visceral intensity of Rich's trading character. "So Rich wanted to screw Jesselson."

"Why?"

"There is one rule in this business," he said. "When you've been fucked over by another trader you retaliate in kind."

By all accounts Jesselson had no idea that Rich and Green were planning to bushwack him and, even if he had caught word of the pair's plan, would not have believed it possible. Jesselson was a consummate trader and a fascinating boss to work for, but he was unable to understand the needs and desires of modern-day executives like Rich and Green, men who no matter the circumstances saw themselves climbing, crawling, inching their way up a corporate ladder with no reward in sight. The world had outgrown Jesselson's style; too much money had caused the needs of his traders to rise faster than his clannish thermodynamic could contain. "The world," Tendler said sadly, "became too ambitious for Jesselson."

Rich and Green began plotting what Philipp Brothers executives would come to refer to as "The Mutiny" around November 1973 in Madrid and Zug. Bravado was the key element because it was critical that their action stun the other in-house traders. Rich wanted to show Philipp Brothers that Ludwig Jesselson was not invincible. He hoped that this would

95

prompt other traders to join his ranks, leaving Jesselson as little more than the shattered figurehead of a company time had passed by. After weeks of secret meetings, Rich and Green put their plan into motion in Zug in February 1975.

Rich traveled from Madrid to Zug, where he met Green to prepare for a meeting of the company's European management committee, a group of senior executives who managed the firm's day-to-day activities in Europe and made recommendations to management in New York. Both men had decided to closet themselves with Jesselson and discuss their yearly bonuses a few hours before the committee was scheduled to meet that afternoon. The pair had created some $4 million in oil profits that year, a figure that would have made them due for the most fabulous of bonuses had they been trading anywhere else. But since Jesselson never based bonuses on any formula, Rich and Green knew that they would have to go in and punch it out with the old man. Rich and Green, however, had agreed that they would throw the fight by asking Jesselson for so much money that he would inevitably refuse and expect the two traders to head on back to their offices with a much lesser sum and no further lip.

The meeting began smoothly. Rich outlined the profits he and Green had accumulated for the firm, and Jesselson listened patiently. "Then they dropped the bombshell," a Philipp Brothers senior executive who was in Zug at the time said. "They wanted $400,000 each in bonuses. Jes probably didn't move when he heard the figure. He loved Rich and I'm sure he thought it was kinda funny.

"Jes said no and Rich became arrogant. He apparently told Jes that he was so out of touch with reality . . . I don't know the exact words used, but Rich attacked him, told Jes that he was no longer capable of running Philipp Brothers. A lot of people here felt that we should be getting more money and knew that Jes was set against the idea. Nobody liked the policy, and we all kept trying to change it. Rich went in there and ripped Jes apart over it. Right or wrong, I don't know."

"The traders at the other houses were all getting a percentage of the profits at the time," Ben Bollag, then a Philipp Brothers vice president, said. "Jesselson felt that if he gave in to Rich he would have to give in to all of his traders. Jesselson's biggest problem was never being able to adjust to the possibility that other people besides him could make fortunes. He always told traders that their success came from having Philipp Brothers behind them.

"The lecture was 'If it weren't for the power of the company which I [Jesselson] built, then nobody would be making any money, and you should be extremely happy with what you are now getting.' Everybody bent over backwards not to antagonize Jesselson. Marc was the first one to do it because he wanted to become wealthier than Jesselson. If there was any hatred, as has been said, then it was directed at Jesselson for holding him back and not at Philipp Brothers as a company."

By the time Rich and Green left Jesselson's office that February morning, every gossip in Zug buzzed that the Philipp Brothers "odd couple" was gearing up to start their own trading firm. Oddly, many traders both in and out of the company hoped the story was false. Ralph Meyer, who had outraged Jesselson when he left Philipp Brothers in the mid-sixties, tried desperately to talk Rich out of the plan. "Ralph told Marc to stick it out because the company needed him more than Jesselson's old ways," a friend of Meyer's explained. "He told him to let Jesselson roll off his back."

"They were part of the Philipp Brothers family and did a lot of good for the company," a former Zug trader explained. He added quickly: "But we didn't know what happened in that meeting or what he had done to Jesselson. All we heard were rumors, and we felt that Jesselson should do everything to keep them here."

"Rich warned Jesselson that he would leave if his demands

weren't met," said Bollag. "Jesselson's arrogance would not allow him to believe it to be true."

"Rich knew before he went in there that Jesselson would never agree to the bonus," argued a Philipp Brothers director. "It was a premeditated plan to hurt Jesselson and sway other traders to leave the company with him."

Any thoughts of keeping Rich and Green were dashed by the start of the management committee meeting that afternoon. "There were two empty chairs in the room," an executive who attended that meeting described. "Marc and Pinky didn't show up. They stayed in their own offices, cleaning them out, I think. The mood was quite tense. Jesselson didn't say anything. Then someone broke the ice by asking if [Jesselson] had made every effort to keep Rich and Green with the company."

Jesselson looked calmly around the room, zeroing in on the two empty chairs. Then his gaze sprayed the table. "I have not," Jesselson responded with deep hurt in his voice. "Those two . . . those two . . ." He paused to catch a breath but ended up sighing deeply, sadly. "Those two," he repeated, "they will destroy the company." Nothing more was said.

A few days later, when the European managers were gathered for their yearly photo, Jesselson uttered the names of Rich and Green for the last time. "Before the rumors start, I want to say that Rich and Green asked for bonuses so high they would break our rules and traditions. They have separated. It's time to close ranks."

Hubert Hutton recalled that the New York office recoiled in horror when the news reached them by phone. "After a while though everyone was glad they left because it became apparent that all Marc and Pinky wanted to do was feather their own beds."

"Their departure," said a member of the European management committee, "had a traumatic effect on the company. All the traders were annoyed that they were being paid such small salaries in comparison with the rest of the industry. It was another signal that Jesselson was no longer able to run the show effectively."

"Many executives felt that Rich was a great loss and privately held the ancient ways of Jesselson to be responsible," Bollag said. "Jesselson was a brilliant man working out of his age. The board was so scared that they'd lose more traders that the very next year the company started to give all the traders exactly what Rich wanted in the way of compensation."

The mutiny had been a great success. Philipp Brothers was thrown into a total state of confusion over Rich and Green's departure, and nobody had any idea what to do. Marc Rich had pinned Ludwig Jesselson the way Lilliputians snared Gulliver. Green began boasting to friends that he had asked for a $1 million bonus, adding more fuel to the New York rumor mill. "There was even talk that Jesselson had a fatal stroke," a trader remembered. Confusion reigned for weeks. Executives didn't know what Rich had taken with him or what he wasn't supposed to take with him or who was to tell clients that Rich was no longer a Philipp Brothers trader. "These were bathroom-key questions and nobody had any answers because we never before had to deal with them," a Philipp Brothers trader explained in amazement.

Rich, the debonair business machine, and Green, the laidback Orthodox Jew who wore dirty shirts and sneakers to the office, departed with six top Philipp Brothers traders, files of information on the company's global network of producers and consumers and, said one trader, "an obsession to grind Philipp Brothers into oblivion at whatever cost." Financing was furnished through a $2 million loan arranged by Rich's father via the American-Bolivian Bank and a $1 million cash injection by Jacques Hacheul, a Philipp Brothers trader who had jumped ship, and a promise from Iranian Senator Ali Rezai to help set up a series of no-holds-barred oil deals that would, in part, lead to making Marc Rich the most wanted whitecollar fugitive in American history.

"They left here with a desire to build up an organization bigger and more important than Philipp Brothers, and that's understandable," a Philipp Brothers director mused. "It was the way he did it that we all grew to loathe," the man added vindictively. "It was patricide, you know. That's really it. Marc Rich committed patricide."

PART III
STRATEGIC DEALS AND DANGEROUS CURVES

CHAPTER 8

"I can't stand it much longer," whispered Tom, in short catches between breaths. Huckleberry's hard pantings were his only reply, and the boys fixed their eyes on the goal of their hopes and bent to their work to win it. They gained steadily on it, and at last, breast to breast, they burst through the open door and fell grateful and exhausted in the sheltering shadows beyond. By and by their pulses slowed down, and Tom whispered: "Huckleberry, what do you reckon'll come of this?"

MARK TWAIN, *The Adventures of Tom Sawyer*

ARTOGRAPHERS have always represented Zug with a diminutive dot on the Swiss map, despite terrain that makes the lakeside town a uniquely attractive location for engaging in corporate battle. Barricaded from the rest of the world with deep forests, treacherous mountains and the most advantageous tax rates in all Switzerland, Canton Zug's 77,000 residents have made their capital town an uninterrupted hermitage for the wealthy and powerful for nearly six centuries. The result, of course, is gold. Zug is one giant vault, with gold assets equalling 13 ounces for every man, woman and child—more than ten times the equivalent per capita gold reserves of the United States government.

Today Zug's reputation is part multinational Hole-in-the-Wall, part Alpine Peyton Place, a secure homestead for thousands of public corporations and private trading firms drawn here with promises of cheap and negotiable tax rates. The town is one huge protection racket, allowing individuals to curtain their affairs behind a Swiss corporation by simply bolting a brass nameplate onto a law office door and opening an

103

account at a bank where discreetly instituted but draconian measures of confidentiality prevail. "We don't ask what they do," said cantonal secretary Dieter Delwing, aware that his is a smug system of sheer inventiveness unable to be transferred anywhere else in the world. History and geography have conspired in these mountains since 1870, when Zug's burghers helped to profitably manage the competing business interests of Bavaria and Baden during the bloody Franco–Prussian War, convincing Zugerlanders to become world specialists in the job of financial camouflage.

The logic behind Switzerland's legendary secrecy laws— *pecunia non olet*, or "money has no smell"—permits the country's heavy dependence on foreign imports to call for unrestricted capital movements across its frontiers. Any attempt by foreign governments to portray Switzerland's laws as an overcoat for crime are discounted as sheer fantasy by its leaders. But a rising share of foreign business, coupled with fiduciary management of private and institutional foreign funds, has transformed Switzerland from a mere laundryman of refugee dollars into the world's finest dry cleaner of soiled money. And Zug is the chain's flagship store.

Although 27,000 people live in the city of Zug proper (the rest are scattered throughout the cantonal villages of Unterägeri, Oberägeri, Menzingen, Steinhausen, Hunenberg, Cham and Baar), over 120,000 work there, hundreds in the business of sculpting corporations that provide the canton's citizens with over $200 million in taxes every year. "The canton gives us a tremendous amount of leverage," enthused Paul Spier, who was a trader with Sasson Metals in Brussels before leaving to specialize in establishing Zug companies for metal traders. "There is nothing negative in Zug. It's a town with no downside." Spier has a singular grasp of the financial needs and clandestine nature of the metal business. He was once a clever and daring metal man until he misread a cadmium market while trading at NICA Metals in 1978. Maneuvering to cut loose from his position, he walked boldly into the office of

Willi Strothotte, a director at ICC Metals who would later join Marc Rich to head the metals and minerals division, turned his back to the desk, pulled down his pants to expose a bare ass and exclaimed, "I can't pay for the cadmium so you better fuck me!" Today Spier answers suspicious questions posed by those who want to set up shop in Zug with total confidence and persuasive charisma, a charming peddler of Zug tax shelters.

"Zug wants anyone with money to be here and they act accordingly," Spier explained, pointing out that less than 15 percent of Swiss real estate is owned by Swiss citizens. "There are only eighty-four work permits issued in Zug every year, and an ancient law states that ten of those must be given to professional foresters. Shall we say that Zug has many foresters wearing suits these days."

Legend maintains that the only numbers published in Zug are in the phone book and that there exists one bank for each of the town's 8,000 corporations. Zug's burghers do nothing to defuse the myth; the fable remains the town's most endearing asset, reinforcing the brazen aggressiveness Zug's leaders use in merchandising Swiss secrecy laws to businessmen the world over. "Zug will always give you a cheaper rate," said a London trader who owns a Zug corporation. "They even invite comparison shopping." The essence of the Zug benediction concerns "transfer pricing," a paper shuffle in which material is transferred between a company's various subsidiaries. This calving, as it's called, can be done legally; however it's illegal for a subsidiary based in the United States to pay inflated prices for material it buys from another of its company's subsidiaries based in Switzerland. The masquerade results in a movement of profits from the United States to Switzerland and the criminal evasion of American taxes.

The cost of setting up an uncrackable Zug shell is minimal. All that's required is a 3 percent stamp duty on share capital, a canton registration fee of $300, a notary public stamp costing $500, and various transfer fees totalling some $3,000. The company has a choice of either headquartering in Zug or paying an independent front man approximately $25,000 a year for a maximum of 150 hours' worth of office work to help certify that the company is a Swiss entity; the shellmen will send and receive telexes, mail letters and sign contracts on Swiss soil, secretarial functions that could cost the phantom owner millions of dollars in taxes if carried out in the country where a deal originated. Boards of directors are composed of cantonal officials, and over the years have included Zug's police chief and chief prosecutor. Zug banks will gladly leverage operating capital against share capital—an officer from the Union Bank of Switzerland suggested that it's best for a metal-trading company to start with $1 million, to which they would seed another $2 million in subordinate loans.

Zug is a paradise for privateers, a Dodge City where the wanted ride limos instead of palominos, shoot with telexes not Winchesters. And the law mandates provisions for dealing with potential Wyatt Earps: Local police have the right to arrest anybody whom they suspect is involved in activities prejudicial to the Swiss economy and hold that person without formal charge for two weeks. "There are no individuals in Zug," said a trader for Fernacom, a Zug-based metal-trading firm, "only private shareholders." The town's most famous shareholder would come to be Marc Rich, who came here with the Philipp Brothers blasphemers in the winter of 1974 seeking to create an empire sheltered and safe from the probes of the outside world.

Rich's first move was to register Marc Rich + Co. AG, a trading firm empowered to transact business anywhere in the world under the protection of Swiss secrecy laws. Headquarters was his cramped apartment in Baar, a small but wealthy village on the outskirts of Zug where Rich would spend his evenings calculating the various ways of destroying Ludwig Jesselson, as the cold Swiss sun set on his competitors' European offices a few miles to the west. Rumors of what Jesselson would do in retaliation drifted through the canton thicker than snow. Talk of wild revenge and destruction filled the air. "Philipp Brothers was not a place you could leave delicately," Hubert Hutton mused, reflecting back on the tense atmosphere that engulfed the trading community in the days following Rich's departure. "The competition was always scared of Philipp Brothers. They'd believe that Jesselson would sneak into their telex rooms at night disguised as a cleaning lady if somebody said it with a straight face. These are the kinds of stories that traders want to believe whether or not they are true."

The most evident truth rolling through Zug was Marc Rich's ability to trade, even with a limited bankroll. He was a superb organizer of people and tactician in the relentless use of a private corporation as a wedge against the ethical restraints imposed by the public sector. If the conquest of Jesselson was his ultimate goal, as many traders from both firms were led constantly to believe, then everyone knew that Jesselson would never surrender Philipp Brothers; it could be taken only by heavy siege. The order of battle was for Rich to swarm the marketplace, igniting volatile markets for oil and metal. Rich's presence as a wild card would put pressure on others scrambling for the same material, fomenting an emotional market situation where a private trader could move easier and profit quicker than one chained to a public corporation. "Marc has the qualities that distinguish the average trader from the brilliant trader," said a broker who competed against him. "When he trades a commodity, he knows its differentials, its qualifications, where it's needed and where it can be gotten. He does that by knowing what's happening around the world and by having an enormous network of people."

The network was small at first and totally dependent on milking deals from Philipp Brothers. The five traders who left the company with Rich were all prima donnas, breakers of the Philipp Brothers mold and accustomed to intriguing business away from the competition. The challenge Rich offered invigorated them like a blast of salt air. Although there was little money to pay salaries, Rich whetted their pirate senses with assurances that they would share in the booty; they followed him with the loyalty of sea dogs, secure in the knowledge that their master would treat them well when it was time to be fed.

Deals were quickly sealed for chrome and copper, both metals that Jesselson had considered himself to be an absolute monarch of since the fall of the Third Reich. Rich's traders were offered huge incentive bonuses if they outwitted Philipp Brothers for material; they wandered the ports of the world like apostles, purchasing loads of lead, tin, zinc, sugar and rice. Senator Ali Rezai, however, was Rich's trump card. The two men closeted themselves in Tehran in early 1974 and worked out an agreement in which Marc Rich + Co. would purchase nearly half of the chrome dug out of Rezai mines in Faryab and Esfandaghe. Rezai was ecstatic. "Ali said it was the best thing that ever happened to him because he could now play Rich and Philipp Brothers off against each other," said one of Rich's metal men. Rich traders claim that one of the earliest scams was to purchase huge amounts of copper and then place the material off-warrant, a paper shuffle that warehoused the metal but failed to list it as registered stock on the world market. Off-warranting gave the impression that the market was short, sparking an instantaneous buying spree among dealers who needed to supply copper immediately and allowing Rich to sell his copper at a premium well above the market price set twice daily by the London Metal Exchange.

"Rich went into Chile in 1974 and bought 5,000 tons of copper concentrates," recalled Fred Schwartz, the tough and outspoken president of Redco Resources, a metal-trading firm. "He just went in there and did it, you know. It didn't matter a bit that he had a built-in loss of $500,000. He did the same thing with manganese in Brazil.

"The guy wanted to make a name for himself in the industry, and it really takes a guy with brass balls and foresight to say, 'I don't mind losing a half a million dollars,' " said

Schwartz, who made his mark as a metal man under gunfire, contract salvaging war scrap off the South Vietnamese coast for the United States Army. "Rich didn't mind blowing what money he had because he knew he'd get a lot more out of it in the long run. He needed to scare the competition, and losing a half a million dollars calmly can start a lot of fucking fear in this business."

Rich's business days began no later than 6:30 A.M. and dragged on until he fell asleep. The telephone became an integral part of his anatomy, and on the rare occasion that one was not glued to his hand, his traders would joke that Rich's wife had had it surgically removed while he slept.

Rich transferred his physical operations into a tiny three-room London flat on Great St. James Street at the end of 1974. Rich and Green sat opposite one another, constantly hollering what deals they were making back and forth across the apartment, causing the rickety walls and floorboards to shake and moan whenever the cries of "Hey, Pinky!" "What, Marc?!" rumbled through the place like blasts from a firehouse claxon. The London office was a madhouse scene and a good deal of fun for the traders who sometimes slept there overnight lest they miss an important telex from somewhere in the world that Rich—who read every telex going in and out of the office—might quiz them on the next morning. The uproar during normal working hours was tremendous, and visitors to the place had no idea how anything could be accomplished. Contracts and telexes were piled all over the flat and phone lines snaked around the room like Vietcong trip wires.

"We were four floors up, and there was no elevator to get us there," a trader who worked there described fondly. "It was so small that everybody had to stand up to make room whenever somebody came into the office. A few of us even had to conduct business from the couch in Marc's office, and he would have a terrible time throwing us out whenever he wanted to have a private meeting."

Rich's presence in London added prestige to the company.

The City was the financial supermarket for international traders, providing easy access to brokers on the London Metal
Exchange and to the big banks who used London as their
center for foreign lending operations (Citibank, for example,
orchestrates $13 billion worth of loans from its London office).
London was also the home of Philipp Brothers' first foreign
office, a fact that did not escape Rich in his decision to become
a major force on the London metal scene. The office was
managed by Felix Posen, a former Philipp Brothers trader
who was given the nickname "Sir Felix" because of his grand
manner. Posen was an American in passport only. He bought
a huge, detached mansion in the Sussex countryside and stocked
it with the finest European art money could buy. He entertained there grandly and was always donating corporate money
to help out the various royal drives to rebuild parts of London.
"It was the old Philipp Brothers system," a Rich trader said.
"Headquarter your European operations in Zug to manage all
transactions taking place outside the United States; base most
of your day-to-day traders working foreign deals in London
and keep the brain trust in New York."

After six months in London, Rich and Green moved to the
twenty-fourth floor of the Bankers' Trust Building on New
York's Park Avenue, and Sir Felix transferred London operations into more modern offices situated on Wigmore Street
in the West End. The new London office was an odd place
for a trading house since it was in the middle of an area
renowned for expensive abortion clinics, fashion showrooms
and surgical supply merchants who decorated their windows
with syringes, scalpels and prosthetic devices. "You'd walk
out the door at Wigmore Street into the most macabre scene
in London," a Rich trader laughed. "Everybody we dealt with
worked in the City and they used to hate coming to visit us.
It made them uneasy."

The New York office was like a sky fortress, a far cry from
what had been a lone trader managing American deals out of
a spare office provided by Rich's father from the day his son

left Philipp Brothers. The latest security systems were installed and each employee issued a special computerized pass with which to unlock doors. All traders were instructed to deposit telexes in an outgoing box for daily collection by a mail room attendant whose job it was to ensure they went through the state-of-the-art paper shredders. At the Zug office shredded telexes were shrink-wrapped in plastic and sold as scrap. Rich's transglobal network was coming together. The frontispiece was New York, the new home of Marc Rich International, the American subsidiary under the protection of Marc Rich + Co. AG, the Swiss parent.

Many of the early deals were carefully hedged back-to-back trades where buyers had already been contracted to take delivery. The trades maintained cash flow and laid a solid foundation for the growth of the company. But they were trades inimical to Rich's temperament: Rich was El Matador, the man who disdainfully viewed caution as a frivolous disease that flourished only in frightened environments. And nothing ever frightened Marc Rich. "Think big was the unspoken rule at Marc Rich," said one of his young traders.

To generate the cash needed to operate on a truly ambitious scale, Rich turned to Pinky Green, instructing him to use Ali Rezai—"one shrewd peasant," Rich would say—to develop schemes of securing long-term contracts for Persian oil above and beyond the normal market channels. For the next three years Green made monthly trips to Tehran, where he toadied up to any factotum with lines to Shah Mohammad Reza Pahlavi. Through Ali Rezai he made contact with Reza Fallah, head of the Iranian National Oil Company, and contracts were signed to provide Rich with a 200,000-barrel-a-day supply of Iranian crude at the height of the oil crisis. "I've never seen Pinky as happy as he was the day he walked out of that meeting," a Rich trader said. Again through his relationship with the Rezai family, Green was introduced to Abolfath Maui, an Iranian superagent and hustler on the Tehran scene who also happened to be the Shah's cousin. Green, Rich and Maui developed barter deals for Iranian oil, including one grand scheme in which Rich would receive oil against money he would invest to help finance a German firm's construction of an Iranian nuclear power plant. And, beyond his own personal greed, the Shah needed all the cash he could lay his hands on to help finance the lofty dreams of the Peacock Throne.

CHAPTER 9

Every moment is a risk.

JACK SWIGERT,
Apollo 13 astronaut

SHAH MOHAMMAD REZA PAHLAVI was a great man for a private trader such as Rich to do business with, despite the fact that the Western trading community never considered the Shah's regime reliable or stable. Rich liked the Shah because he grew most cooperative whenever the time came to raise the price of oil on the world market. When Rich began doing business with Iran in 1974, the country had the capacity to pump nearly 7 million barrels of oil a day. Such figures looked good on the surface and served the Shah well in becoming a powerful force in the Gulf region until he was toppled by Ayatollah Ruhollah Khomeini in 1979. But from the moment Pinky Green first arrived in Tehran, Rich and his senior oil staff knew that the Shah owed $3 billion in foreign debt as early as 1975 and, more important to Rich, Iran's debt was rising much faster than its income, prompting the Shah to jump into the Eurodollar market for dollar loans. In ironic despite of his vast oil wealth, the Shah was cash short, a trading situation devilishly structured for what one of Rich's Middle Eastern oil traders called "funny business."

"We spent a lot of money in Iran paying for introductions,"

a senior Rich oil trader explained. "The question is really what constituted a bribe. We gave vacations to government officials with lousy salaries both in Iran and in countries such as Angola and Nigeria. We helped their families with cash and took care of their business expenses. This was considered a matter of good business and convenience." But the arrogance of Rich's cash opened oil pipelines that had been closed to others. Iranian crude was sold to Israel, Royal Dutch Shell, and Elf, the French oil corporation. Rich installed Gerard Demanget, a Frenchman, as his oil man in Tehran. The appointment was on the surface a curious choice, since Demanget had previously represented the French automotive company Citroën in Iran and knew absolutely nothing about trading oil or metal. "He was a public relations man and Marc hired him because he knew whom we needed to pay off to get into Iranian oil," a former Rich executive said candidly. "Gerard was our front man and he grew very rich."

Rich's Iranian oil deals were extremely sweet and allowed him to glide above the oil apocalypse of the 1970s, particularly during 1976 and 1977, when oil imported to the United States hit its peak, constituting nearly half the petroleum consumed by the American public. If the going rate for a barrel of OPEC oil was $20, then Rich would purchase it for $15 and then sell it at whatever the spot market would bear, a figure that changed daily, sometimes hourly, and was always significantly higher than the OPEC price. And although OPEC was a powerful cartel that maintained a series of quotas and price structures that looked good on paper, the day-to-day business of oil was conducted in a vacuum in which none of the major oil companies knew exactly how much oil flowed onto the world market. "It was good business for us since we didn't have to put up the cash until the oil was sold," a Rich oil trader explained. "Money paid on the side always helps close a deal, but Marc had a way of convincing people that they should sell only to him. The man could lie through his teeth and people would believe him. Then Pinky would crawl into their hearts, and we had them. They were fantastic to watch.''

The Iranians were happy to wait until Rich had sold their oil on the spot market or through independent deals with the majors before collecting their money, especially since he made meticulous provisions for kickbacks from the overprice sales to be placed secretly into foreign accounts. "The Iranians, the Nigerians, anyone who did oil business with us liked to keep a portion of their share in the West," said a Rich oil trader who claims to have deposited $125,000 in cash into the coded Swiss account of Reza Fallah, head of the Iranian National Oil Company, in return for "services rendered" on securing a shipment of Iranian crude destined for Spain in 1977. "The Iranians were corrupt as hell and paying them off has been the only way to do business there for 5,000 years. To go into places like Iran and do honest business is naive. I'd figure 15 percent of your net in payoffs for every deal made. You got the business, and that's what you're there for.''

Rich became so big in oil that he seemed to appear like a Saudi sheik wherever there was an oil deal to be made, often to the embarrassment of the American oil companies. Big oil, which was used to purchasing crude directly from the producing nations, squirmed when dealing with Rich. He had become a prickly thorn they could not remove because of the nationalization of foreign wells: When Exxon wanted access to oil in Marxist-controlled Angola in the late seventies, executives set up a meeting with the country's oil agents. Expecting to receive a politburo of Angolan officials representing the Malonga oil installations in the northern province of Cabinda, senior Exxon oil men—loath to deal with the former Portuguese colony since its embrace of communism after the Portuguese departed under a hail of gunfire in 1975—were visibly stunned when the communist representative who walked into the conference room turned out to be Pinky Green, greeting Exxon executives with a hearty "How ya doin'?"

One of the tools Rich used to hammerlock Third World oil supplies was a flashy multimedia show depicting the history of the petroleum business from the day Colonel Edwin Drake sank the first well in western Pennsylvania. "The concept was to convince these leaders that they could grow richer if they dealt with us," a Rich oil trader said. "The show was quite effective. When we showed it in Angola, the country's leaders brought their wives, families and all the relatives. The film was a night on the town for these people."

While oil prices continued to surge, Rich lined up contracts that supplied 200,000 to 300,000 barrels of Nigerian oil a day to be resold on the spot market at premiums spiraling as high as $14 a barrel. And when Iran started cutting off supplies to the Western companies, the oil firms became desperate. "We had to scramble because we lost 200,000 barrels a day overnight," Martin Volandt, Arco's senior vice president for crude supply, said in an interview. "We tried to buy Nigerian, but we were unsuccessful." Arco, like many of the other oil giants, was forced to go to Rich, who had a contract with Nigeria and middle-manned the crude to Arco at a fat premium.

Arco, the seventh-largest American oil company, was Rich's best customer. Rich had become close to Arco trader Bill Ariano while still at Philipp Brothers and referred to his buddy in telexes as "Crude Bill," instead of the usual telex code of "Crude Arco." Rich had first supplied Ariano with Nigerian crude while manager of Philipp Brothers' Madrid office. Ariano's son Michael was given a job in the Rich organization. Rich went as far as to name a tanker after Ariano's wife, Jeanne, inviting the family to Tokyo for the christening ceremony.

The *Billy Jeanne A* was the latest addition to the Rich fleet, which already comprised the *Devali I* (named after Denise Rich and Green's wife, Valerie) and the *Mediterranean Sea*. The ships, however, were not in the greatest of shape, and on one occasion the *Mediterranean Sea* docked at Arco's Philadelphia terminal in such pathetic condition that inspectors deemed it a fire hazard and made it leave port. Such inconveniences were tolerated because if Marc Rich told an oil company he had oil, he had oil—so much oil that his spot trades to domestic oil companies regularly took first prize in the weekly office pool at the Department of Energy, where workers would guess which American oil giant would pay the highest spot price before the figures were released officially. The marriage of the metal men and the oil barons was cozy but one-sided. Throughout the seventies the oil companies said that they had to charge the consumer higher prices to finance new oil exploration to lessen America's dependence on OPEC production. Although a great deal of money was invested in exploration, a lion's share went into the mining, manufacturing and exploration of minerals—a $10-billion-a-year enterprise in the United States during the late seventies. Exxon had invested $1 billion in the La Disputada copper mine in Chile; Arco shelled out $700 million for Anaconda; AMOCO bought into the Cyprus Minerals Corporation; Penzoil invested heavily in molybdenum and copper; SOHIO assumed a piece of Kennecott Minerals; and Mobil gobbled up a giant's share of Falconbridge nickel operations.

It was crystal clear to Rich that the oil companies were becoming very interested in metals, particularly copper, where American oil companies controlled 40 percent of the domestic copper industry and held major interests in six of the thirteen largest copper mines in America, accounting for 95 percent of domestic production. The oil companies managed their metal-trading operations poorly, the trading mentality being far removed from what the Seven Sisters were accustomed to. And whenever Exxon, Arco or Royal Dutch Shell had a question on how to handle a metal position that they had no idea what to do with, they called Marc Rich. "It happened all the time," said a Rich trader once in charge of purchasing oil from Venezuela. "No one in business likes to admit that they don't

117

know what they're doing. The oil companies had no business in the metal trade. They were never equipped for it. I was more than happy to advise them, to our advantage."

Profits for the first five years of Rich's operation were huge: $14 million for 1974, $50 million for 1975 and over $200 million for 1976 and 1978. Swiss tax records for 1979–80 indicated a total pretax bonanza of $367 million. And that was only the money for deals through Switzerland. Said former Zug Mayor Walter Hegglin of the Rich money machine: "As long as Marc is doing all right, Zug is doing all right."

The profit door was Iran. "That's how we moved our position so fast," said one of Rich's traders. Although much of the operating capital was plowed back into purchasing more oil, millions were earmarked to smother Philipp Brothers' bids for long-term contracts to control Philippine copper concentrates, Brazilian pig iron, South African ferro-alloys and Jamaican bauxite. Ore and oil were resold as quickly as possible, except in the United States, where the material was warehoused and a nationwide distribution system created to sell crude to refineries and metal to foundries directly. But it was foreign oil that powered Rich's industrial juggernaut. By the first quarter of 1976, he had fifteen oil traders buying and selling oil in Sweden, Norway, Russia, East Germany, West Germany, Switzerland, France, Italy, Spain, Israel, England, Malta, Turkey, Rumania, Yugoslavia, Austria, Libya, Algeria, Nigeria, Morocco, Zaire, Gabon, Sudan, Angola, Mozambique, Ethiopia, South Africa, Japan, Singapore, the Philippines, Malaysia, Brunei, Iraq, Iran, Dubai, Saudi Arabia and all of North and South America.

The minimum oil deal Rich would touch was 100,000 tons, and that was rare. The bulk of Rich's profits came from charging staggering premiums to oil companies short on their production quotas. One of the biggest was in 1978–79, when Rich negotiated two contracts with Arco to supply 40,000 barrels a day. Twenty thousand of those barrels were sold at an $8-a-barrel premium over Nigeria's official $24-a-barrel price. The remaining 20,000 barrels were sold to Arco at $5 over the official price. Future contracts between Rich and Ariano would charge premiums and commissions of $3 and $2.50 a barrel. Arco ultimately bought 27 million barrels of Rich's Nigerian crude, fetching $120 million in commissions and premiums. But it was still a good deal because spot prices for Nigerian oil were marked higher than what Rich was selling his Nigerian oil for. Rich and Green grew giddy over the oil deal profits. Green, recalled a member of his staff, "pranced around the New York office applauding himself after he swapped fourteen Boeing 747s to the Saudis in return for oil that he was going to sell to Israel." Another trader added: "Marc went everywhere chainsmoking Monte Cristo torpedo Havanas, the fattest and most expensive cigars in the world. He was on top of the heap. It was magic."

Magic, like everything else in the trading world, is a negotiable commodity, the cost usually proportional to the level of a producing nation's corruption. Payoffs to secure material were code-named "chocolates," and every Third World leader with whom Rich did business seemed to have a sweet tooth. When unseen market forces intervened, more chocolates had to be delivered, as was the case with a shipment of Nigerian crude out of Lagos in 1978. "We told the Nigerians that their oil had been going to Spain, and one day they followed our ship twenty-five miles out of port and saw it hang a left instead of a right," a Rich trader laughed. "A lot of the Nigerian oil had been sold to South Africa at a huge profit to us, and when the Nigerians found out they canceled the contract. It cost us a million chocolates to get the contract back."

The $1 million payoff, allegedly paid to Alhaji Umaru Dikko, Nigeria's transport minister and the obsequious brother-in-law of then President Alhaji Shehu Shagari, was one of dozens of bribes disguised as surcharges to fix traffic violations and serve as partial down payment on a long-term $12 billion deal that would supply Rich with 100,000 barrels of Nigerian oil a day. The Shagari regime personified corruption in the Third World, and Marc Rich was there to help add to the mayhem. "Marc never once reflected on the moral implications of a deal," one of his senior executives explained. "Doing business with corrupt societies was exactly the same as doing business with anyone else. I don't know if that's right or wrong. What I am sure of is that it's business."

Tam David-West, a former university professor who became the energy minister of Africa's most populous nation after Shagari was overthrown in a New Year Eve's coup in 1984, estimated that over 20 percent of Nigeria's oil revenue from the mid-seventies until 1983 was lost through fraud or smuggling, helping to nurture the country's $24 billion debt to foreign banks and international loan institutions. And Rich's trades for oil were not limited to just cash. Rich traders concluded deals that swapped grain for Nigerian crude, but once staples such as rice and wheat reached the Lagos port, Dikko put the food through a circuitous system of payoffs, inflating a 110-pound sack of rice that cost $35 dockside to $267 in the markets, the difference lining the pockets of Dikko and Shagari's National Party. "What we did was dangerous to a degree," warned one of Rich's African oil specialists. "Marc never *worked* with the countries he did business in. He played off of them and he always knew that he stood to get screwed if he lost the upper hand."

Rich always managed to walk a thin and menacing tightrope between the profits of business and the powers of politics, particularly in the South American nation of Ecuador, one of his major suppliers of crude oil outside the OPEC price structures. Ecuador stopped selling oil to Rich in early 1978 after the company failed to come up with $10 million for a disputed oil cargo. But when oil prices went up even further a year later, Rich returned to Ecuador with the $10 million and brewed a new series of contracts that swapped weapons for oil. The deal had all the ingredients for an explosion. At that time Ecuador was involved in a border war with Peru, another country that supplied oil and minerals to Rich. Neither country

complained. Ecuador needed guns and Peru needed hard
Western currency. Rich supplied them with both.

The money from the oil trades also caused an infection
known as Richophobia, a disease that was spreading faster
than a winter flu virus throughout Philipp Brothers. The four
major private shareholders of Marc Rich + Co.—Rich, Green,
Hacheul and Alexander Hackel, who was the only member
with a valid Swiss work permit—had an obsession with ran-
sacking their former firm for telex operators, receptionists,
secretaries and traders. In New York former *lehrling* Hal Beretz
(an usher at Rich's wedding who went on to become president
and chief operating officer of Phibro-Salomon and a director
at both Philipp Brothers and Salomon Brothers) was secretly
offered a $2 million cash incentive just to leave Philipp Broth-
ers and join Rich. Beretz declined. In Buenos Aires Philipp
Brothers officials claimed they captured a Marc Rich trader
paying bribes for Philipp Brothers' telexes; in Tokyo they
caught a Philipp Brothers trader who was acting as a double
agent for Rich, the spy snared by a Philipp Brothers trader
who was dating a Marc Rich secretary. "Secretaries and clerks
were asked if they had a problem sleeping with their clients,"
a former Richco Grain executive explained. "Secretaries and
other low-level personnel were always zooming off on business
trips they had no reason to go on. The company paid for their
jewelry and furs. Anything they wanted."

One of Rich's most successful ploys was to find "lost sons"
who were disgruntled over being stationed in faraway places.
His gambit was to offer them twice their current salary and a
new position wherever they wished to be stationed. The catch
was that they had to stay in the place they wanted to leave
for six months and establish the local Marc Rich office. Rich's
intelligence on Philipp Brothers seemed uncanny. William
May, a member of the Phibro-Salomon board of directors,
alleged that Rich's fifth column electronically bugged the phone
system in Philipp Brothers' New York headquarters and that
debugging experts had to be called in to sanitize communi-

cations by analyzing voltage drops and sending tracer signals along the wires to locate taps.

The guerrilla raids were enormously successful; corporate loyalties had a way of losing their durability when cash entered the equation. Rich offered traders three to four times what Jesselson was paying and a piece of the long-term action. Top traders were given upwards of $500,000 a year plus bonuses. Nearly 100 people received stock that had to be cashed in upon leaving the company. Even Rich's personal secretary, Ida Levitan, a valuable ally in obtaining Philipp Brothers gossip, was given shares in the company, a move that outraged traders who had no connection with Rich's former bosses. Rich's senior staff was instructed to "fuck over" Philipp Brothers; Marc Rich secretaries were urged to "date" the competition's traders. "Anything was possible if it screwed Philipp Brothers," said a trader who had an opportunity to observe one raiding party. "Rich wanted to get his hands on a Jamaican aluminum trader who had some sort of Philipp Brothers connection. The trader was flown from Kingston to London, driven to his penthouse hotel suite in a Rolls and arrived to find naked hookers prancing around the room. Women, cocaine, cash—it didn't matter as long as Philipp Brothers was put out of business." In aluminum the plan worked. By 1977 Rich had become the biggest aluminum trader in the world, snatching bauxite and bodies away from Philipp Brothers.

No Philipp Brothers employee was immune to Rich's enticements. Traders were snatched away to form one-man outposts, often located intimidatingly down the hall or across the street from the Philipp Brothers office from which he had been taken. Whenever a Philipp Brothers trader left to join Rich, he brought decisive information on the competition and placed it at Rich's disposal. Some of Rich's more successful strafing runs against Jesselson took place in Bolivia, a Philipp Brothers stronghold since the thirties. Whenever a contract came up for renegotiation, Rich traders would inevitably bid a few cents higher than Philipp Brothers. This would go on and on like a broken record, Rich always offering just a few cents more than Philipp Brothers had offered moments before for tin, bismuth and tungsten. "They were beating our bids for metals by a fraction on every one," a Philipp Brothers trader lamented angrily. "They knew our bids before we did."

For his part Jesselson arranged meetings with Philipp Brothers suppliers, attempting to persuade them not to deal with Rich. Meetings with mine owners and producers in South America, Africa and the Far East were futile; Rich's adventurous repartee was just too good. The more remote a production area was, the more Rich people seemed to show up in an effort to secure it for what many traders perceived as a fearsome rebellion against the time-honored traditions of Ludwig Jesselson's way of business. "Rich shocked the hell out of Philipp Brothers," said a Philipp Brothers banker at Samuel Montagu, a London bank with a long history of extending credit to the company. "Until Rich came along, Jes had created his own safe little world with no competition. It was comfortable, protective and extremely profitable. The psychological effect Rich had on Philipp Brothers was devastating."

The arrival of a Rich emissary to marshal material openly angered Jesselson but delighted producers accustomed to bear markets who could now juggle competing bids to make even more money. Jesselson's anger stretched beyond the trading room and into the family kitchen, where those who did business with Philipp Brothers found their knuckles being rapped once Jesselson discovered they were also horsetrading with Rich. After he heard that Rich had become a client of Ropner Insurance, a London firm with a long history of taking huge risks to insure Philipp Brothers cargo, Jesselson, out of pure spite, say traders, changed insurance companies. "We wanted to do business with Rich," said a former bullion trader for Philipp Brothers in London. "Jes wouldn't allow it. There were no memos sent around saying 'Stay away from Rich'; it was understood. And it wasn't good business for us to keep away from Rich. We could have made money off Rich. The only thing you had to watch out for was that Pinky returned all your fingers after shaking on a deal."

Emerging like a thunderclap on the world market, and harboring a visceral desire to intimidate Philipp Brothers wherever possible, Rich growled whenever anyone insinuated that he hired people to learn what went on inside Philipp Brothers. "They are crazy," he would sneer, adding quickly, "Jesselson just can't admit that some of his people might think that I'm a better boss to work for." Like clumps of weeds, Rich offices sprouted up without warning throughout the world. By the turn of the decade, Rich commanded forty offices in thirty countries, brandishing over 1,000 people to seize control of large caches of strategic commodities essential for manufacturing goods as disparate as breakfast cereal and jet fighters.

The total net worth of the company was $1.5 billion, two-thirds of it resulting from the long-term oil contracts Rich liked to conclude with a firm and dry handshake. Rich traders estimate that by 1980 sales were in the $12 billion range, the profits channeled through an international hydra of some forty-eight secret companies peppered throughout the Netherlands Antilles, the Cayman and Bahamanian islands, Liberia, Lichtenstein and Panama—all linked ultimately to Marc Rich + Co. AG, the Swiss parent. But Rich's favorite financial haven was garreted two flights above a greasy spoon on London's Tudor Street, the British home to the consulate of the Republic of Panama.

Paint peeled from the walls of the office, and the stench of burned bacon and oil-fried eggs hung heavy, but this foul-smelling place represented a cathedral in the Marc Rich empire, the place where he sent companies to be cured of the affliction known as taxation. Sitting behind an old wooden desk, underneath a tattered map of the Republic of Panama, is a lynx-eyed secretary with the ability to help an international trader extinguish his tax burden by creating a Sociedad Anónima. "May I please have information outlining the formation, operation and taxation of corporations under the laws of the Republic of Panama?" one needs to ask.

Smiling pertly she will hand the trader a thirteen-page document and say: "You can choose your own name to be incorporated, or I can provide you with a selection of titles already incorporated in Panama. When you make your decision please return with $1,650."

Only cash is accepted.

Rich traders indicated that Marc and Pinky washed money through numerous Sociedades Anónimas, many of them with nonsense names like Highmans Consultants and Rescor Incorporated. Using a Panamanian corporation in his portfolio, Rich could conduct legal business transactions in any country, have a small percentage of his profits declared as taxable income (to avoid government scrutiny) and pay the rest to the Panamanian corporation, whose real owners are sacred secrets under the laws of Panama. The corporate money can then be dripped into any number of foreign banks whose bylaws also ensure secrecy. Directors of a Panamanian corporation are, quite often, other corporations—some even Panamanian—created for the sole purpose of providing another blanket of protection against the chill of scrutiny. Panamanian corporate law is particularly helpful to a trader whose operations extend outside the Central American nation and into several different countries. A Sociedad Anónima is never required to file financial reports or tax returns and may maintain its books in any manner it desires in any part of the world. This permits a procedure generally known as laundering, and for Marc Rich—an expert at sidestepping the politics of nations by acting as a maverick middleman between producers and consumers—it was quite the bargain at $1,650 plus a $50 annual franchise tax.

"There was over $800 million in pure cash floating around the companies at the time," said a former Rich shareholder who maintained that Rich would relieve boredom by "starting up" another Panamanian company. "The interest alone on our accounts at Bankers Trust, Chemical and Paris-Bas was paying for salaries and overhead. There was so much money that we had bankers lined up in our hallways asking to borrow our money."

"There is always a way to make money on a deal if you are in total and absolute control," Marc Rich would lecture his traders. "Always have total control and you will survive and you will make money . . . anyone can sell a dollar for 99 cents." Within eight short years Rich's mineral rites had exorcised most of his demons. It was a liturgy of total power, executing a global commodity colossus that sold more oil than Kuwait, more copper than Chile, more grain than the Dakotas and enough aluminum to wrap the British Isles in foil. The deals were Byzantine in complexity, and the details were known to him only. Rich's world became a bewildering prism; he could refract and displace billions upon billions of dollars through dozens of countries and companies and pockets until they, like light, finally disappeared from view.

Suddenly the entire trading fraternity was talking about Marc Rich's disturbingly ingenious assaults on the world marketplace. Rich was drawing attention, and trading tradition dictates that conspicuousness is undesirable, possibly dangerous. But the slightest reference to any Rich involvement in a negotiation uncharacteristically exhausted, frustrated, befuddled and dazzled the traders, especially the younger ones. Doing business with Marc Rich was laced with exotic mystery, implacable suspense and huge profit. What was true? What wasn't? No one but Marc and Pinky could ever separate the fact from the fiction. The hustle was clever, empathetic and perfect to run against men who subsist chiefly on rumors. The skinny was clear: Marc Rich was on his way to becoming a cartel and, grumbled the executives at Philipp Brothers, he was doing it at the expense of his alma mater and the delicate instability of the metal-trading community.

CHAPTER 10

"An oil camp's no kindergarten. There's no room in this world for people who don't look out for themselves. What do we care about people? All that matters is oil."

B. TRAVEN, *The White Rose*

A RUSTY FENCE was all the protection between the factory compound and the pedestal-mounted .50 caliber machine gun Tony Garcia had bolted to the floorboard of his jeep. The ground was still damp from the spring rain, causing terrorized workmen to slide out of control as they scrambled for cover behind bulldozers, automobiles and reservoirs of ore waiting to be smelted into chrome. No one remembers how many armed men bounded out of Garcia's two trucks and the cab of the earth scooper, but he deployed them in a phalanx in front of the motorized column.

Garcia jumped from the jeep and nodded to the man behind the .50 cal. Other than the metallic slap of the breech locking the ammo belt into the World War Two relic, related an observer, the assault started in silence, punctuated by slow motion bursts of activity.

The place was outside the town of Cagayan d'Oro on Mindanao, the southernmost major island of the Philippine archipelago and body to some of the Earth's richest veins of chrome ore. It was 1981 and Tony Garcia—who supplied the

Philipp Brothers upgrading facility with ore harvested from his land—was ready to spray his clients with reprocessed lead. The relationship between Garcia and Philipp Brothers had been free of problems, a winning example of the company lending money to develop a mine in return for marketing rights.

Like many other Filipinos, Garcia had acres rich in mineral deposits but not a peso to use in digging out his wealth. So Philipp Brothers drew up contracts that gave letters of credit good for an immediate 10 percent of the mine's estimated production. Garcia used the cash to purchase equipment and as a down payment on the 15 percent of the mine's net value demanded by the Marcos family, who controlled a piece of whatever was dug out of Philippine soil. Contractual problems had always been solved under the friendliest of terms, prompting workers at Cagayan d'Oro to ask themselves why they were looking down the wrong end of a machine gun.

Garcia claimed that Philipp Brothers had not paid him for 200 tons of ore piled on the other side of the fence and that he had come to collect it. Peter Cutfield, Herve Kelecom and Bambi Castillo, the three Philipp Brothers traders in Manila, had no idea that their client was so upset. "If he only had called," Kelecom thought bitterly. Garcia, however, was not in the best of moods. Screaming, he informed the guards, some workers and two apparently mush-witted policemen called hastily to the scene that if the gate was not opened he would come through the fence, shooting anyone attempting to stop him from leaving with his ore. A guard obligingly opened the gate. One of the trucks plowed through the fence anyway; the policemen smiled, hands in pockets. Luckily, not a shot was fired. The chromite was loaded on the trucks and the convoy sped off, Garcia vowing to plant officials that Philipp Brothers had not heard the last of this matter. Still no one had any idea what Garcia was raving about.

Over the next few weeks, Cutfield began receiving threats against his life, forcing him to send his wife and family out of the country and to spend his nights in a series of hotel rooms, accompanied constantly by bodyguards. "Everyone at the office began sleeping on edge after what happened," a trader explained. David Tendler, who served as the company's former Tokyo office manager with expertise in the Far East, was sent to Manila to discover what led to Garcia's alleged theft of Philipp Brothers' material at gunpoint. No one had a clue. "The people in New York were madder than hell at Marcos for letting this happen," said a Philipp Brothers trader in Manila at the time. "We had paid Garcia for the chrome. It was ours. The situation was such that all we could do was stop doing business with him."

Tony Garcia stayed in business, the 200 tons of Cagayan d'Oro chromite finding its way aboard a Marc Rich freighter, according to a Philipp Brothers trader who methodically dogged the ore's movement off the islands. "It's impossible ever to know if Rich had anything to do with what happened on Mindanao," said Herve Kelecom. "Anything and everything was possible with Marc Rich."

Though the Mindanao skirmish was downright bizarre (Garcia bargained wisely and remained in the Rich camp), the jungle drama reinforced Rich's reputation as the enigmatic Action Man. Trading was a matter of style, and Rich held the monopoly on grace under fire. The real beauty of a Rich trade was that Rich, the master dealer, and Green, the master mover, could purchase and ship material without the knowledge of anyone else in the company because all information was supplied on a need-to-know basis, a policy that further clouded the full extent of their global trading activities. "Making money was the chemistry of the friendship between Marc and Pinky," a friend of both men said. "Traders build a myth around themselves to sell their wares. Jesselson had done it, and now Marc and Pinky were doing it. The best traders are myth builders. Marc and Pinky understand that."

"This business is about creating situations, and that's exactly what Rich knows how to do," advised Trader Robbins, a director of Unicoal, one of the many metal-trading firms Rich did business with over the years. "The deal is what's really important. You can always find money. But you have nothing unless you have a deal to go along with it." Rich's style became the most advantageous element in any trade. The dark eyes, focusing hard and stubborn like shooter marbles, made people worry about what he was going to do next but anxious to be in on the action. His 6-foot frame—timid and shy, curved slightly at the neck and with the long arms of a third basemen tough to bunt against—was decked out in the sleekest of expensive suits and garish $50 silk neckties that, traders guffawed, would make a comfortable noose if he hung himself on a deal.

Rich considered himself too much of an acrobat ever to stumble over a situation of his own making, even in Iran, where the Ayatollah Ruhollah Khomeini had deposed, exiled or murdered the Iranians who made up his oil network. By the beginning of 1980, the Rezais had escaped to New York City, Houston, Los Angeles and Costa Rica; Fallah flew to the safety of his Swiss bank accounts; Maui fled to London, and the Shah died of cancer in Panama. The Peacock Throne was rubble and Khomeini was exterminating the insiders who greased its corruption like so many flies. The American hostage crisis only added to the twisted theatrics taking place within Tehran's Western trading community. The greatest liability for a trader now doing business in Tehran was his life. Every trader in town pulled stakes and ran for cover—everybody, that is, except Marc Rich, who took out ads in *Metal Bulletin* to tell the fraternity that he wasn't going to be run out of town. "It blew the trading world away," said John Hughes, a director of LHW Futures in London. "Everyone raised their eyebrows over that because it didn't seem right, you know. It was a wild west show for him."

Rich told Gerard Demanget to stay put and to make sure that he dodged the bullets on the way to the office because there was business to be done. Rich figured that Khomeini—

who had just overthrown a government that depended on petroleum for over 90 percent of its export income—needed to sell oil just as badly as the Shah and that he could probably purchase it cheaper since President Carter and other Western leaders had instituted a trade ban against Iran in reponse to the American hostage seizure. There was one hitch: To trade with Iran was now a criminal offense, possibly high treason against the United States. A few of his traders warned him that the public, at the very least, was against any American's doing business with Khomeini's gang of Shiite thugs, including many people in Rich's own office. Rich and Green viewed criticism of their plan to do business with Iran as a sign of weakness. Rich turned to his years in Spain to help formulate a plan. Torkild "Cap" Rieber, the gutsy boss of Texaco during the thirties, had shipped $6 million worth of oil on credit to General Franco during the Spanish Civil War. And when Franklin Roosevelt threatened him with indictment for violation of the Neutrality Act, Cap Rieber sent Franco Texaco oil through Italy. Franco won the war, Rieber grew fatter and Roosevelt soon forgot about the whole matter. Marc Rich would do the same thing, except he would buy instead of sell, filtering payments for the Iranian crude through Marc Rich + Co. AG, his Swiss company. Rich, confident that his plan would succeed, ordered Demanget to start buying oil from the new proprietors of the Iranian National Oil Company . . . take them out to lunch.

The daring endeavor paid off, Rich insiders indicating that the company paid for much of the Iranian oil in weapons—particularly small arms, automatic rifles and hand-held rockets shipped across the Indian Ocean from Thailand and through the Suez Canal from Spain. "My impression was that any arms deals were conducted by Rich and Green alone," advised a senior Rich executive who worked in London during the hostage crisis. "The procedure would have been for us to purchase weapons outside the United States or act as the representative of a foreign manufacturer."

"You would have thought we had our own pipeline into Iranian wellheads," said one of the Rich managers who monitored some of the oil deals with the Khomeini regime. "We bought millions and millions of barrels from Iran during the hostage crisis. When the price of oil went up to $40 a barrel in the fourth quarter of 1980 we were paying around half the world price in Iran. Rich got more excited than I had ever seen him."

"Marc dealt his way out of the Iranian revolution by taking his life in his own hands," said Hubert Hutton, his former colleague at Philipp Brothers. "If anyone was capable of screwing over Khomeini, it was Marc. He knew how to do that."

The trades grew grander in style, richer in bounty, potentially deadlier in execution. When on the hunt, Rich was the consummate charmer. He entertained at his lavish oceanfront home in Lido Beach, Long Island, or in his Park Avenue apartment that once belonged to cosmetics queen Helena Rubinstein. Limousines were dispatched to collect clients for intimate business gatherings catered by the finest chefs money could buy. Green, who rarely ate anything other than melon and black coffee, stayed in the old Brooklyn neighborhood, entertaining his clients over fat pastrami sandwiches at the best kosher delis in Flatbush. But no matter where he was, the cigars were only Havana, the port certainly vintage, the grand designs always combustible.

One of the characters on Rich's international bandwagon was Yuri Igorov, a tough-nosed senior executive of Raznoimport, the Soviet firm that buys and sells metals. Until 1979 Raznoimport had operated solely as an agency marketing strategic Russian metals to the West, with Rich a major overseas buyer of titanium, lithium, cadmium, vanadium, manganese and a giant's share of the platinum-based metals used to manufacture the components used in sophisticated weapons and computer systems. Raznoimport's Kremlin bosses knew the company could generate more hard Western currency if they embraced capitalistic markets as both a buyer and a seller of material. Igorov approached Rich to help fortify a London office where Raznoimport could base their Free World metal trades. Rich, a major purchaser of Soviet oil, rolled out the red carpet.

"We took real good care of the Russians when they came to London," one of Rich's European traders related. "We bought them breakfast, lunch and dinner. Our limos and cabs drove them everywhere in London. We put them in touch with solicitors, accountants and Western businessmen who could help in creating the British corporation. We did everything for them.

"One of our staff was told to help Yuri find a flat to live in. We thought it would be no problem since the Russians don't care how much a place actually costs. Turns out that Russians living abroad are allocated a certain number of square meters of living space in relation to their position. Not one estate agent we contacted knew how to figure out square meters so we had to go around London doing it for them. These guys from Razno would come into the office wearing dirty raincoats to pick up someone to go help them figure out how many square meters were in a flat. It went on for weeks because Yuri wouldn't accept a square meter less than what Moscow said he was allowed."

CHAPTER 11

To survive in Hollywood you need the ambition of a Latin American revolutionary.

BILLIE BURKE,
wife of Florenz Ziegfeld

ARC RICH needed a tax shelter. By 1981 his various trades in the United States had sucked in more money—an estimated $1.2 billion in pure cash alone—than many banks controlled: It was a problem that needed speedy action. Rich discussed his cash overload with Marvin Davis, the president of Davis Oil, one of the largest freelance oil operations in America. "Rich and Davis knew each other from a few joint ventures they made drilling for domestic oil," a senior oil executive at Rich said. "Davis taught Rich everything he knows about the domestic crude business."

Davis, a hulking 200-plus-pound wildcatter from Denver who made a fortune digging high-risk wells, convinced Rich that Twentieth Century-Fox would make a nice tax shelter. Rich drew back. Owning a movie studio wasn't the kind of low-profile investment he'd had in mind. Studio bosses were in the public eye, and that was the one situation Rich could not afford to let happen. Rich's wife, Denise, thought it was a wonderful idea. She was not the kind of woman to just sit at home raising their three daughters. While in New York she opened a fashionable boutique on Madison Avenue and spent her spare time writing and singing songs. "Denise wanted to be known in society, dance under some limelight," said a Rich executive who knew her. "Marc was too secretive for her taste. She wanted to get out and do the kind of things a woman with money can do. They were very much in love, but Denise just wanted a chance to strut her stuff and not have Marc deal with her like he did with people at the office."

Davis, who had until then been plotting to take over Fox by himself with some $650 million he acquired from the sale of Beaufort Sea oil wells to whiskey manufacturer Hiram Walker Inc., put the pressure on also because he needed the tremendous leverage Rich had at the banks. "Marvin didn't have the necessary money to do it on his own," said an insider to the deal. "If he'd had the capital, he wouldn't have asked Rich." On the surface the buy-out looked good to Rich. Fox owned an Australian theater chain, the Coca-Cola Bottling Company of Minneapolis, a new network of home movie and videocassette distributors, interests in Pebble Beach Properties and Aspen Skiing Corporation, and a sixty-three-acre studio lot in the heart of Los Angeles. "Marc saw all this and decided Fox was a real estate deal," explained a trader who discussed buying the movie company as a tax shelter with Rich.

Rich was ready to bite, but only if he could be a silent partner. Davis agreed. Rich formed a Netherlands Antilles corporation called Richco Holdings to purchase 50 percent of the voting stock of TCF Holdings, a private holding company created by Rich and Davis to acquire Fox in the spring of 1981, and to serve as a repository where any profits could be split. In June they formally purchased the company for $725 million. Some $550 million of the purchase price came through lines of credit Rich arranged through a group of eight banks led by Continental Illinois National Bank & Trust Company of Chicago. Rich paid the other $175 million in cash. His ownership of the giant film studio remained secret for six months. "Marc got real nervous when everybody found out that he was the mystery owner," snickered one of his senior oil executives.

The irony was that nobody in Hollywood had ever heard of Marc Rich and attempts to discover who he was resulted in dead ends. Davis, on the other hand, was a well-known figure who had made no secret about wanting to add Fox's lucrative nonentertainment holdings to his portfolio. But unknown to Fox at the time of the purchase, Davis was also keenly interested in making creative decisions on scripts and casting. Marvin Davis wanted to be a movie star. The Denver oilman—a genuine film addict—was enthralled by the Hollywood spotlight and made frequent visits to the Fox lot, eventually purchasing a $21 million (paid mostly in cash) Beverly Hills estate dubbed "The Knoll." The 25,000-square-foot home, set on ten acres with guest cottages and garage space for fourteen cars, was a movie mogul's Xanadu and a vivid indication that Marvin Davis, at least, intended to be a very visible studio boss. Rich, however, had little taste for his partner's public romance with Hollywood and went so far as to refuse a seat on the captains-of-industry-and-politics-studded board of directors.

But the moment word spread throughout the trading community that Marc Rich owned Twentieth Century-Fox, his customers started calling from all over the world. Rich couldn't believe what was taking place—calls from the Nigerian Oil Ministry asking for a dozen cassettes of *Star Wars* and an advance cassette of *The Empire Strikes Back*; a telex from a Brazilian metal supplier asking if his son could meet C3P0. Rich thought he had purchased a real estate company but soon found out that he owned a piece of George Lucas, the most popular moviemaker of the day, and *M*A*S*H*, the most popular television series in history. "Marc realized that buying Fox was the best thing he ever did for the trading department," one of the oil traders laughed. "Everybody loves the movies."

Rich directed his traders to let it be known that any customer who wanted videocassettes of Twentieth Century-Fox movies or TV shows need only to ask and they would be delivered. Foreign offices in the Third World were instructed to tell local politicians that Marc Rich was now in a position to help them get deals on movie equipment and would be more than happy to send teams of experts to develop fledgling film industries. "I juiced up an African oil contract by telling an oil minister that if they underpriced me $4 more a barrel I'd have Fox come make a film in their country," said one of Rich's oil dealers. "Marc thought it was great for business."

Marc Rich was not the kind of studio mogul that Hollywood was accustomed to, but his credentials made him ideally suited for the job. Trading commodities, like making movies, was a speculative venture rooted in human fantasy and susceptible to grand illusion. The movies dramatized people's fantasies; Rich delivered on them.

Rich cast Fox in his own movie, used the studio's assets to help package and perpetuate his own myth. He developed relationships with members of the Fox board, men like former President Gerald Ford and former Secretary of State Henry Kissinger, men he would never approach unless in total command of any situation that might develop from the rapport. In Kissinger he saw a man born to Hollywood and bred in Washington. He was the consummate character actor, always striving to usurp the role of star. Scripts mattered little to Kissinger: The destruction of Cambodia with carpet bombing, the overthrow of Salvador Allende in Chile, and his attempt to upstage Joan Collins when he made a cameo appearance alongside her on the soap opera *Dynasty* had made him prime time's most popular star. Kissinger was a believable myth, manufactured under government specification, ready to be molded, manipulated and traded like any other commodity.

Kissinger's first visit to Rich's office is believed to have taken place after a morning screening of *The Verdict*, a Fox film, in early 1982. "Marc called him 'K,' and to see them together you'd think they were childhood friends," said a former senior Rich executive who was first introduced to Kissinger by Rich in 1982. "They both came from the same background and they shared an interest in what was taking place around the world. My impression was that Marc just picked his brain for information not generally available. He always grew excited after meeting with Kissinger."

Kissinger made at least ten visits to Rich's office. Sources indicate there were dozens of phone conversations between the two men. The meetings were always between Rich, Green and Kissinger, held in Rich's private office and segregated from the rest of the staff. On at least two of those visits, Kissinger brought along copies of his books, *The Years of Upheaval* and *The White House Years*, and autographed them for members of Rich's staff, including Rich's secretary Ida Levitan. Like a spider encasing flies in webbing, Rich slowly wrapped Kissinger in his intrigues. "Marc was a real sucker for prime ministers and presidents," reflected an oil trader who met Kissinger while he was in Rich's office. "He would use anybody."

CHAPTER 12

You can't underestimate the power of fear.

T HE HUB OF Rich's amazingly effective organization
was his *lehrlings*, all young men motivated by money
and who would do anything for it, no matter how
ridiculous or dangerous. It wasn't necessary to have
a trading background to work at Marc Rich. Hiring anyone who possessed "tomatoes"—Rich's euphemism for tes-
ticles—he transformed holiday travel agents ("they can
move anything") into traffic managers, Madison Avenue glad-
handers ("they know how to manipulate people") into metal
traders, and the blood relatives of his directors ("they know
how to keep their mouths closed") into office managers.

"Marc preferred people who could speak a language besides
English," one of his former shareholders related. "But it always came down to whether or not a guy had tomatoes. He'd
tell the staff and the people we did business with that they'd
never be screwed if they had tomatoes. 'If you got tomatoes
then we can make a deal.' "

The opportunity to deal with fascinating people, the fantastic salaries, the chance to manage offices in faraway places
and a mandate to pursue whatever business imagination could

139

conjure up served as glamorous recruiting incentives for dozens of young men. At the other trading houses, inexperienced dealers were usually relegated to the purgatory of a back room, but at Rich the gifted could race as far and as fast as their guts could carry them.

Prospective employees were interviewed first by Rich and then by Green, both men firing detailed questions on any friendships they might have with traders at other commodity houses. "He despised people who had friendships with competitors that he could not in some way benefit from," a trader Rich hired from Associated Metals explained. "He always asked if the friendship was really necessary."

"He told me I could develop any business that I thought had potential," a junior trader said, recalling his interview with Rich. "He warned me that I was out the door if I talked about our business to anyone outside the company."

"I never encountered such a stimulating environment in my life," one thirty-two-year-old trader boasted of his five years working for Rich in New York, London and Latin America. "I was twenty-five when Marc hired me . . . man, the trading world knew I was part of the crème de la crème."

Life inside the Rich organization had the sensitivity of a jackhammer on an open sore. Traders began to sense that their world would go to pieces or become hopelessly dull if they stopped traveling wildly like roving linebackers. Distasteful excesses were encouraged if they helped conclude deals. Life for many traders became a dangerous and massive fascination with the out-of-control power money can buy.

"It got to the point where I couldn't go out after work without a $400-a-night prostitute on my arm," one of Rich's junior traders brooded. "I was twenty-six and the whole business was driving me out of control. All the young traders in London had money. You didn't have to work for Rich. But the guys at Rich were encouraged to out-finesse the competition, even if they were our friends. We paid for the cocaine, we paid for the champagne and when we were at metal con-

ferences we paid the brothel bills. It was madness. The logic
of it, and I'm only guessing, is that we might pick up some
obscure piece of information that might be profitable for Marc.
I never really found anything that would make him that much
richer. I suppose there were those who did. Many of the guys
were afraid to talk so you never really knew. It was part of
the paranoid scene."

"A member of the Inner Circle once told me to take a lot
of petty cash to take some of our South American customers
out for whores," another former Rich metal trader said. "It
made me sick. I came back the following morning and told
my boss that I would never do that again. I knew right there
that my career was over at Marc Rich."

Business was inspired through fear and intimidation. Traders referred to Rich and the other principals who founded the
company as the "Inner Circle" and the "Jewish Mafia," ag-
onizing that they would be caught in an elevator alone with
any of them. The office became a synonym for tension. Mar-
riages broke up and traders ran off with their secretaries because, said one trader, they were the only ones who could
ever understand. Rich didn't care what happened as long as
the job was done, the trade concluded. "And boy, you better
have the answer if Rich asked you a question because they
knew everything that was going down in that office. It was
scary."

The emotional cost of a deal was never taken into account.
All that mattered was staying on top of the deal, constantly
reappraising the market and remaining on twenty-four-hour
call to brief Rich, Green or the Inner Circle. "Everyone at
Marc Rich was greedy," said John Hughes, who knew many
of Rich's European staff and once briefed Rich on possible
real estate investments. "They were so cocky that they thought
their next deal would be for the nails that put Christ on the
cross.

"A lot of their traders became unrecognizable because Rich
kept moving them around so fast. Everyone who knew a Rich

trader felt abused in some way. They all thought it was a glamorous lifestyle to be hopping on planes to Brazil with twenty minutes' notice, but they all suffered a loss of trust. You never heard businessmen say 'fuck' so much in your life. They were constantly 'screwing somebody' or 'ramming it up somebody's ass.' It was a perverse form of business."

Rich had moved from the Bankers Trust Building and now observed his world from the penthouse of the Piaget Building, a ritzy Fifth Avenue skyscraper financed in part by his friend the Shah of Iran. Over a million dollars was spent to decorate the reception room—"the place had more mirrors than a New Orleans whorehouse," said a trader. Internal stairways linked floors together, and Rich filled his office with electronic gadgets that made the place look like "the bridge of the starship *Enterprise*." The Piaget offices were run like a supersecret military installation. Nothing was allowed in a trader's office unless approved by Rich personally. "He didn't like anyone eating in their office or putting their own pictures on the wall," said one of his former employees. "I once saw him explode because a trader put his feet on the desk. He said, 'Would you do that to your own furniture?' He went nearly berserk."

Documents, scraps of paper and personal belongings were to be swept off desktops whenever an outside visitor or client entered a trader's office. Rich made spot checks during office hours and haunted the corridors like a banshee after work, making sure that everything was either locked up or destroyed. "There was a constant fear of being caught at something," muttered a trader, commenting on the paranoia level in the New York headquarters. "Marc would call you into his office for a meeting in progress, and you knew that he wasn't telling you everything that you should know. He wrote notes in letters so small that you could only read them with a magnifying glass. Once he was done with you, he had no problem in telling you to leave the room. We always walked out scratching our heads, wondering what was really going on.

"Very few things made him laugh. He used to have problems working all the electronic stuff. He'd push a wrong button and TV sets would appear, bar doors would swing open and lights would start flashing all over the room. It made his office look like Studio 54, and people would always ask him if he wanted to dance."

Rich's ability to unnerve the formidable men who made up his trading staff was the inevitable result of the money he paid. "It was business by example," said a trader who spent six years on his payroll. "Marc wanted everyone to act as he acted. We noticed that Rich never went to the bathroom without a handful of telexes so we started going to the bathroom with telexes. It was an absurd scene, men holding telexes with one hand and directing their piss with the other to impress the boss."

But the traders knew that Rich rewarded dedication with cash, and home loans were easier and cheaper here than at the bank. Whenever a trader concluded an impressive deal, he received a congratulatory telex from Zug (where the final contracts were signed) that was read by both Rich and Green. "It was the star on our foreheads," said one of Rich's young traders. But like everything in the Rich empire, the Zug telex portended a dark side. "You never knew whether or not Rich was happy with you. He never said anything until the annual review. You could warp your brain waiting for that."

Rich's annual inquest into a trader's performance was a horrible experience, even for seasoned metal men. Traders were called without warning by Ida Levitan, Rich's secretary, and told to appear immediately in her office. There they would sit, squirming like school kids waiting to give testimony to their principal. "You'd wait sometimes an hour for the guy ahead of you to come out of Rich's office," a trader explained. "That scene would have made a great commercial for underarm deodorant."

Numbed after the long wait and grinning nervously as Rich's door opened, the trader walked in to meet Rich's stare grinding coldly into his eyes. Rich's desk, of course, was bare except for the trader's personal file, which he opened slowly for dramatic effect. "You wouldn't be working there if you weren't good," said a trader. "There was nothing to get upset about. But you did. Rich intimidated the hell out of you before he ever opened his mouth."

Executives were never "fired" from Marc Rich—just ridiculed and disposed of quietly by Green, the corporate hatchet man, to some menial traffic job or paid off to keep their mouth shut once they left the company "under the friendliest of terms." Like everything else in the Rich empire, the policy of silence at any cost often reached extraordinary proportions. Rich once grew so deliriously mad over a pricing error committed by one of his junior metal traders that he convinced a competitor to hire him, with Rich—unbeknownst to the trader— paying half of the salary. "The guy didn't know enough to hurt us," a former shareholder explained, "so the offer tantalized the competition."

The inimitable trademark of a Rich man was the ability to rearrange reality for the company's benefit. The ambience of the Rich trading room was that of a magician's stage, a place where silhouettes accounted for more than exact images. Like the sorcerer directing his apprentices, Rich expected his traders to disorient audiences, cultivate their trust, hypnotize their instincts. If executed properly, the technique was marvelous. But to some of the men who made up Rich's trading illuminati, it was like asking clients to be ripped off.

Jack Wollman did not look like a crook, a distinct advantage in a world where first impressions mean everything. Wollman—a senior traffic manager—was a heavyset suburbanite with a stucco house on Long Island, a head of thinning gray hair and a collection of Corsican briar pipes that he loved to chew while walking around the New York office, giving him the look of a tenured university professor. "It was hard to believe that Jack was an embezzler," said a Rich trader.

In early 1981 Rich called Wollman on the carpet and accused him of stealing nearly $3 million since 1978. It was a neat

144

trick. Wollman allegedly palmed the cash by drawing a set of bogus charter parties, the deeds traffic managers write between shipowners and merchants to move material around the world legally. The forged charter party—with a higher freight cost—was shown to Rich for approval. But Wollman executed charter parties with lower freight costs and pocketed the difference. Rich also accused Wollman of skimming cash out of the corporate account by withdrawing money to pay for nonexistent imbalances in freight payments. "Jack had no idea that he had been found out," said a Rich trader who worked with Wollman for three years. "Marc called him into his office and told him to have his resignation on the desk in fifteen minutes."

Another event that threw Rich into a rage occurred in Malaysia in 1981, a time when the state-owned tin company, Malaysian Mining Corporation, was suffering from plummeting tin prices on the world market. The sultans of Malaysia elect one of their number to be king for five years, the most powerful among this group being Sultan Mahmood Iskandar of Johore, an independent-minded butcher who commanded a private militia and was convicted of culpable homicide only to be pardoned by his father. The king was Ahmad Shah, the obstreperous Sultan of Pahang, who under the constitutional monarchy could block legislation and declare a state of emergency. The Islamic nation was politics as sheer confusion, the perfect arena for Rich's picadors.

Rich's man in Malaysia was David Zaidner, a Philipp Brothers trader who had left the company to join Amalgamated Metals Corporation in the late sixties after getting in trouble over the purchase of a huge cargo of Bolivian tin that turned out to be alluvium, a sludgy casserole of sand and rock. A slender Egyptian Jew who bandied a Swiss passport, Zaidner was one of the hottest "tin shooters" in Southeast Asia and South America. It was a crap shoot tailor-made for trouble: While dealing tin for Amalgamated in the early seventies, Zaidner was called on the carpet for allegedly bribing the

145

buffer stock manager of the International Tin Council—a sort of tin pot OPEC—to release artificially low tin reserve figures in hopes of causing a market scramble. At first Rich didn't want to hire Zaidner but was talked into putting him in charge of the firm's Malaysian operation by Felix Posen and Pinky Green.

What ultimately convinced Rich to hire Zaidner as a senior executive in the corporation was his expertise in the Singapore-Thailand-Malaysia tin concentrate scam, a kind of shell game in which Thai and Malay tin concentrates were smuggled into Singapore without the knowledge of the International Tin Council. Once the concentrate arrived in Singapore, a group of highly sophisticated tin dealers, many working out of crumbling shanties, purified the tin by running the concentrate through crushing machines. The dealers would then package the tin in steel drums and find a shipping company willing to supply false documentation, an easy task in Singapore, according to metal traders.

World trade in illicit tin concentrate is enormous, accounting for some 10,000 tons of material a year with an estimated market value of over $40 million. Although the trade is conducted frequently in Malaysia and Thailand, the end product is always shipped out of Singapore because the city-state does not consider tin concentrate a controlled or dutiable item. Since the Lee Kuan Yew government collects no revenue on the material, dock inspectors always look the other way when it comes to tin concentrate. Though no law is being broken, the tin concentrate scam creates an artificial imbalance in world supply—a perfect situation for Rich's daredeviltry.

Zaidner was close to the Malaysian finance minister Tengku Tan Sri Datuk Razaleigh Hamzah, and Dr. Mahathir bin Mohamad, the country's prime minister. Without Rich's knowledge at first, the trio embarked on a bold plan to purchase every pound of tin they could get their hands on, stockpile it in Singapore and elsewhere and hope to push up the world price. The Malaysians were extremely eager to go along with the scheme because the country was the world's largest producer of tin and in serious financial trouble over low prices and unable to convince consuming nations or the International Tin Council to provide price supports.

The tin-hoarding operation began in July 1981, roiling world tin markets overnight. The cost of tin on the London Metal Exchange ballooned from a low of $4.33 a pound to nearly $7.50. Tin consumers were in shock. Between March 1980 and July 1981, the price of tin had tumbled from a high of $8.65 a pound to the $4.33 figure. Prices were expected to continue sagging because of a poor economic outlook in the housing industry, which along with cans, was the major use for tin. But now a strange new force had entered the marketplace, prompting consumers and producers of tin to hastily schedule a meeting in Geneva. The Malaysian government, now on a roller-coaster ride, refused to discuss their involvement in the spiraling prices.

The cost of tin continued to zoom upward until January 1982, when it was shot down by the United States government's selling tin from the federal stockpile for a lower price. Prices collapsed by March, falling 22 percent in the last two weeks of February. Rich took a $60 million bath because he had believed Zaidner's tales of even higher tin prices. The Malaysians lost $150 million and were stuck with 60,000 tons of unwanted tin.

Zaidner left Rich soon after that fiasco to start his own company in Zug. He was due for a bonus and cash on liquidated share capital reportedly totalling some $50 million. Rich gave Zaidner only $10 million, teaching him a valuable $40 million lesson in how not to manage a market. "Rich's feeble attempt to corner the world tin market was a dumb move but not a real disaster because he eventually traded himself out of the position at a profit," a veteran Southeast Asian metal trader explained. "People in this business are stuck with tons

147

of unwanted material every day. Rich made a deal, like a lot of us do, that didn't work. What's important is that he made a deal, and a rather large one."

In Rich's world, trading was an obsessive process unable to be contained. Once the details of his deals, true or apocryphal, were removed, the froth of indictments and accusations leveled against him by his friends and colleagues blown away, what remained was a man who needed to trade in the same way that a soldier needs war or a child needs toys. The hunt meant everything to Rich. Not to have it was to have nothing at all.

"Friday was Marc's day to sulk," one of his senior oil traders said sadly. "There was never any business to be done after 5 o'clock, and Pinky had gone home for the Sabbath. Marc would just sit there in his office, drinking his whiskey and phoning around the world looking for someone to do business with. He looked so lonely sitting there. It was only when you saw Marc like that that you felt sorry for him. He didn't have anybody to play with."

CHAPTER 13

When imaginations begin to skid out of control so do
events.

GENERAL ALEXANDER M. HAIG, JR.

"BLOOD . . . everywhere you looked there was blood,"
the concierge muttered, annoyed that the gen-
darmes had sealed the apartment for too long, causing the Mediterranean heat to bake the blood into
the walls he had to clean. "They left him tied up like a
sausage, you know."

Until the morning of April 27, 1983, no one in the trading
fraternity knew the exact whereabouts of E. O. H. "Edmond"
Mantell—Marc Rich's chief operative in Thailand. Mantell
had been missing in action since January. Vanished. The questions about what became of the Prussian trader with a whiskey-
red face, stork legs and a nasty disposition were answered at
7 A.M. that spring morning: He was discovered dead in the
lime-colored bathroom of an unfurnished apartment in Eze,
a medieval village carved out of the French corniche, a few
dangerous curves west along the coastal road from Monte Carlo.

The only other thing that everybody who knew Edmond
Mantell agreed upon was that he had been tortured to death.

Mantell was a virtuoso China hand who went to work for
Rich after nearly twenty years as the representative for Thys-

sen Steel and later Associated Metals in Bangkok. He was a permanent fixture on the Bangkok trading scene, having been transfixed by the delta city from the moment he first set eyes upon the banks of the Chao Phraya River as a young German trader in the early sixties. He was never great as a trader, say those who knew him well, but he stayed in the business because he never complained about being a "lost son." Fluent in Thai and a few Chinese dialects, Mantell worked Southeast Asia like a veteran prospector panning constantly for gold, working far upstream, a wilderness man trying to find the ultimate outcropping. In the process he became an expert on conducting business in Southeast Asia, the Pacific Basin and China. On the day President Richard Nixon announced normalized relations with China in 1972, Mantell was the first corporate American representative to arrive in Beijing to do business, a city whose eccentricities he knew well from the days he spent there as a trader for Germany's Thyssen Steel. Within hours of his arrival, he had purchased a load of tungsten and made arrangements to secure a long-term tungsten contract for Associated's American consumers.

Mantell's strong point was his wizardry at countertrade—a popular Third World procedure in which a merchant helps his customers increase exports of other products to offset the money spent on purchasing weapons. Southeast Asian customers were often treacherous mountain warlords who exported anything from antimony to opium in order to secure arms. There was nothing irregular about metal men dealing in arms, particularly since the materials that make a good antiaircraft gun often make a superior golf putter. Since the day Andrew Carnegie and Alfred Krupp first converted their steelworks into armament factories to produce armor plating and gun barrels instead of steam engines and railway ties, men such as Mantell, who supplied the raw materials necessary to manufacture destruction, had a vested interest in ensuring that the armorer's wares reached market.

Southeast Asia's major arms off-ramp was Bangkok, a mysteriously opaque city where *nagas* and *garudas*—mythical serpent deities and bird-man progenitors—displaced the Western notions of reality. Business in Bangkok was conducted on streets and in brightly colored rooms guarded by eerie-looking sentinels chiseled from magical stones. Interspersed in every arms deal was a rogues' gallery of Western expatriates, Shan mountain opium generals and assassins said to be trained to swallow their tongue in suicide if captured by the competition. Bangkok was a city of ghosts, of supernatural agencies with inexorable appetites for dragging people to their doom. But Mantell relished the desquamative existence Bangkok offered —a man infected with the fury of its backwater climate, addicted to nights rummaging through cheaply bought thrills offered by the 250,000 prostitutes who decided that flatbacking and round-heeling in the musky sex hotels was more profitable than stoop-laboring in the rice paddies.

Such knowledge, however, was essential to grasping the bewildering business dynamic of Thailand and figuring the best way of milking profit out of the fifty-year succession of fourteen coups, fifteen prime ministers and forty-four cabinets. Business in Thailand was linked inextricably to negotiating with the military, the dominant force in the country. Mantell understood that Thailand's barracks had never been united and that it was good sense for a Thai general to maneuver himself into a position of power by purchasing his own cache of weaponry.

Edmond Mantell was the candy man, a Rich field agent who managed to stabilize sensitive situations through promise and payoff. Thailand, Malaysia, Burma, China—the country or the conflict mattered little to Mantell as long as Marc Rich wanted to create a situation. He was a frequent visitor to Hong Kong and the Peninsula Hotel on Kowloon Island, spending his afternoons brokering arms and metals in the hotel's famous marble lobby while the cream of Asian society sipped 4 o'clock tea alongside tired American tourists relaxing in comfort after two-week package deals to the Great Wall. A heavy and melancholic drinker, he often rode the Star Ferry across the choppy bay to drink at the Captain's Bar at the Hotel Mandarin with Western traders preparing to visit Chinese metal merchants on the mainland.

Mantell knew how China worked better than Pearl Buck did and downed more fiery shots of Kweichow moutai with the country's industrial leaders than did any Western economic attaché. He never missed a Guangchou Fair, the industrial forum held every spring and fall in the Chinese city formerly called Canton. Before train and plane services were initiated between Hong Kong and Guangchou, Mantell chugged up the Pearl River in a motorized junk and crossed the frontier by mule cart to buy or barter for freighters of tantalum, wolfram and low-grade silicon. "Edmond was not your usual troubleshooter," one of his colleagues from China explained. "He was always grumbling that he got the shit assignments. After a few drinks he would start boasting that he could put together any kind of deal but that his bosses would never let him."

Mantell never carved a niche for himself in the Inner Circle boardroom because he didn't have the ingenuity necessary to formulate the grand deals Rich loved. He was a bureau chief, an executor who materialized Zug-created situations that were based on local market information he had filtered to Rich via telex. His flaw was an imagination that allowed over twenty years in Bangkok to mislead him into believing that he owned the capacity to manipulate his connection with Zug to wheedle the Orient's powers-that-were into helping him create his own situations outside the Marc Rich group. "The last time I saw Edmond, he was drinking heavily and was worried about a deal he was working on," said a tungsten trader who had drunk highballs with Mantell in Bangkok in late 1982. "He wouldn't talk about it, but from the look on his face, I'd say he was frightened about something."

Mantell apparently fled his sixth-floor office in Bangkok's Chongkolnee Building in January 1983, flying first to Germany and then traveling to Monte Carlo in early April. Mantell and his wife, Hildegard, moved into a temporary apartment on the Monaco waterfront until his Eze condominium could be furnished. His days were spent drinking in cafes along the Côte d'Azur, and he often drove to Nice, where he dined at the trendy Chantecler Restaurant in the Hotel Negresco along the Promenade des Anglais. Why he left Bangkok so quickly was a popular topic of conversation among the friends and business associates he left behind. No one had a good answer.

"He probably woke up one morning and saw himself in the middle of something that he had no control over," remarked an English trader who had dealt closely with Mantell for twenty years. "You just don't leave Bangkok overnight. It doesn't work that way unless something went sour. Bangkok is the nastiest place in the world when something goes wrong."

Four months later Edmond Mantell was dead, the body discovered by a concierge who used his passkey to let in the man who had arrived to deliver furniture to the ground floor duplex Mantell had bought a few weeks earlier. The ordeal had swelled the body out of shape. The murderers had first bludgeoned Mantell selectively with wine bottles and a telephone. He was picked up and flung repeatedly into the living room wall like an uncontrolled battering ram. The force of the thrusts gouged the wall. Tracks of curdled blood on the brown shag carpet indicated that Mantell was dragged into the bathroom, where he was scourged with more wine bottles and loose toilet fixtures. Plastic-coated copper wire from an alarm system that had yet to be activated was jerked from the wall and spun around the limp torso as if it were a casting fly. The police said the knots were professional.

Probably the last thing Edmond Mantell ever did was moan; his mouth was stuffed with wallpaper, coarsely textured and with a floral design. The body was left alongside the tub. The coroner indicated torturing commenced around 7 P.M. and that Mantell died around midnight. Ritualistic killings in Bangkok were designed to leave an intimidating message, but in the

153

tourist village of Eze, it was simply a murder that people wanted to forget about quickly.

Six months later Interpol arrested two Swedish men outside of Stockholm. Newspaper deliveryman Jan Kare and kitchen maker Mikaël Grönhall, both in their early twenties, were charged with the murder of Mantell, whom they claimed first to have met drinking on the afternoon of April 26. The prosecution contended that Mantell had lunched with his assassins in Monte Carlo. Then, for reasons unknown, they accompanied Mantell back to the Les Jardins de l'Ibae apartments at dusk in their victim's Volkswagen Rabbit. After more drinking at the apartment, the trio walked into Eze to drink further at a cafe overlooking the corniche. They returned to apartment 314 a little before 7 P.M..

Concluding their systematic flogging of Mantell, the pair stole the Volkswagen and sped east to Monte Carlo, where they dumped the car, caught a westbound train to Nice and checked into a cheap hotel. Two days later Kare and Grönhall arrived back in Sweden. Police traced them through the hotel registration forms. The official police report discounted the murder as being sexually oriented and stated that Mantell was a victim of indiscriminate violence, probably as the result of drunkenness, because there was no evidence to indicate that the murder had been motivated by anything else. But investigators said privately that Mantell could have been the target of professionals, left to die after being tortured for information. "The beating seemed too well thought out," said a policeman who viewed the murder scene. "Someone wanted to know something."

It was never clear what the two Swedes were doing in Monte Carlo or why they accompanied him to a totally bare apartment. A French policeman who investigated the murder indicated privately that there was one curious twist to the trial. In a Swedish court because of a reciprocity agreement with France, the defense astonishingly asserted that Kare and

154

Grönhall—who gave no reason for their atrocity—did not actually murder Mantell because the trader didn't die officially until two hours after the Swedes left the apartment. The Swedish court bought their plea and handed the two men sentences of five years each in prison.

To the metal men who knew Mantell, his death suggested that negotiations with Marc Rich once settled with handshakes were now being settled with hit men. "It never made any sense," an Associated Metals trader who knew Mantell emphasized. "Strange that he was killed by two Swedes. The Swedes have more business interests in Thailand than any other country. Edmond used to broker Krupp arms to the Thais through some Swedes. Funny." Those who believed Mantell's death to be nothing more than the work of psychothugs observed that he never liked drinking alone and that his death probably resulted from a drunken argument. Although the truth may forever rest somewhere in between, the event added more drama to the Marc Rich legend. It was not so much that Mantell—a heavy drinker with a history of being an exceptionally rude and morose individual—had been killed, but that nobody in the gossipy metal world knew any of the details. "It was a real mystery," said a senior Rich trader, who added that the murder was a sour topic of conversation in the New York office and that all questions directed to Rich about what happened to Edmond Mantell were answered with one of his icy stares.

The most popular theory, according to interviews with Mantell's associates in Bangkok and his colleagues at Marc Rich, was that a Mantell-brokered deal blistered when Mantell demanded that a group of Thai admirals return a portion of the money he had paid for a load of faulty hand-held surface-to-air missiles. Exponents of this hypothesis point out that it's quite often necessary to deal with a Swede at some point if a trader wants to smuggle something into or out of Thailand. "Many of us were left with the impression that Edmond was

155

in trouble because of a botched arms deal and Marc left him out to dry," a Rich trader in New York explained cautiously. "It unnerved the entire office."

Detailed reasons for Mantell's death will probably never be known, but like all things in the trading world, the event was more important than any motivating truth. The story was that Edmond Mantell was dead, murdered violently in a French village where he had escaped to avoid some horrible Bangkok fate. Even if the death was an accidental murder, it was yet another inevitable result of working in the world he played in. Rich's traders were known for their unrestrained behavior and, if the deal warranted, the ability to go to any lengths to create a situation. "If you open up your vest," said a trader of Mantell, "you have to expect getting a knife shoved in." Men like Mantell fed the Rich myth, both in life and in death.

Mantell's burial also amplified the questions that many of Rich's younger traders had been asking themselves for years. By the late seventies there was little delight and a great deal of heaviness associated with working for Marc Rich. "The problem was that the company Rich created grew too big too fast," one of Rich's former shareholders explained. "Marc had lost all touch with reason to such an extent that he believed only his decisions to be the right decisions."

To his credit Rich established a nearly perfect team of traders, but it was also becoming apparent that some heavy-handed generals were emerging from their ranks. New recruits, hired for their flair and enthusiasm, were growing increasingly disgusted by the exploitive manner in which Inner Circle bosses such as Manny Weiss, Paul Wheeler and Danny Dreyfus managed their deals just to keep Rich content. "Many traders urged Marc to split the place up into smaller units where individuality could best be taken advantage of," said one of Rich's senior executives. "Marc wouldn't listen, and it was ironic since he left Philipp Brothers because the power there refused to listen to his ideas." Malcontent traders didn't complain too loudly over what was required of them. Far from

156

it: They were Rich's obedient servants, proportionately loyal to their salaries and trying constantly to argue that their psychic exhaustion could be overcome with another shot of whiskey or a purer line of cocaine.

"There was something wrong with the way we were living," said a Rich trader spikily. He is thirty-two years old, but with a brow that looks plowed by a tractor and hands that shake like tin lids on violently boiling pots of water. "I was twenty-five when I went to work for Marc. It wasn't the drugs or the pressure that got to me. All the young guys he hired could handle that better than the older traders. The problem was a lot more basic: What the hell were we doing with ourselves to make this kind of money? The lifestyle was terrific, but you could never throw the feeling that it could blow up in your face at any moment. No one in the office wanted to hear about it because no one had an answer."

CHAPTER 14

The whole world is about three drinks behind.

HUMPHREY BOGART

THE HIGH-PITCHED motion of a Marc Rich office unnerved even young traders accustomed to the fast
lane. They had all been hired to make money for
the company, of course, and as long as they continued to electrify profits, then Rich did not care if they refused
to embrace the traditional temperance most major corporations
demanded of their employees. Rich's attitude resulted from
a keen knowledge of the tension associated with trading. Unlike the owners of other commodity firms, Rich never bought
the argument that the trading profession was a young man's
game. Rich believed that the money he paid traders cushioned
any psychic or physical pressure and that a trader with enough
cash in his pocket should be able to trade forever, not burn
out by the age of twenty-nine. So it was okay if a Rich trader
needed to wire his brain as insulation from pressure, but only
as long as the trader made money. And making money for
Marc Rich was never a problem because the rules Rich lived
by all but gave traders a license to print any major currency.

"Traders at Rich liked to explain how they could bribe
foreign officials without having to go to jail," said John Hughes

of LHW Futures. "They were extremely proud of their ability to pay off despots with impunity because Marc Rich was a private company and was not under the same bribery regulations that hindered companies after Lockheed got caught bribing people to buy airplanes. Rich's people loved to boast how much money there was to be made if everybody could bribe."

The day-to-day cash flow of the Rich empire came from metal contracts secured through floor brokers or consumers who accepted a trader's guarantee that he would be able to find the metal when it was time to deliver. Absent the metal, a trader is obliged to pay his customer the difference between his offered price and the actual market price—the pernicious "margin" that rules a trader's very existence.

Nearly all the metal Rich traded was consigned to the 200,000 square meters of warehouse space owned by the Rotterdam firm of Steinweg, the largest warehouse operation in the world and the place where orange pekoe tea was born when a warehouseman left a load of oranges atop a shipment of Oriental tea. Although a trader's metal rarely left Steinweg or another warehouse unless sold to a consumer, warehouse managers transferred 70,000 tons of commodities a week, much of it in the form of ownership documents moved strategically like paper chessmen between companies. Knowing how much metal he had, how much he had paid for it, and where it was at any given time were the most important elements of a trader's day.

"Most of us ended up trading because there was no other business for us to go into," one of Rich's *lehrlings* explained. "It was the same at all the commodity firms. They needed young people with no experience whom they could train, but we were very different from the traders who hired us. The traders in my crew protested the Vietnam War, smoked dope all through college and graduated as hippies. We were wanderers without work. Then all of a sudden we packed in the fantasy world for making a lot of money. Becoming a commodity trader was the only option. You didn't need a business degree, just some gambling smarts and a lot of strength."

"Making eighty grand a year when you're twenty-six and having your boss tell you that he's going to hide part of it in an offshore account for you really strokes the ego," said a trader who helped pay his Manhattan rent by dealing pound parcels of marijuana before entering the Marc Rich traffic department. "You could do anything as long as you produced deals. Money was no object. We'd put cocaine, women, cars, records, anything on our expense accounts. Nobody cared. After a while it began to dull the senses. You wanted out, but no one could ever bring themselves to leave. Rich was a drug."

The fellowship born of this cultural confusion was an informal group of ten traders who called themselves the Heavy Metal Kids. The Kids—all hotshot traders from Marc Rich, Wogen, Brandeis, Mercer International, Derek Raphael, Tower Metals and Associated Metals—were founded after they lost money on a cadmium deal instigated by Klaus Busch, a trader for Mondial, a German metal firm. Busch had been promoting cadmium heavily and brought his pitch to London, where he entertained a few traders at Miranda's, a Carnaby Street strip joint known for scantily clad leather girls flogging drunks with velvet whips. By the third round of drinks, Busch began complaining that a major market for antimony trioxide—used in automobile batteries and as a fireproofing agent—had vaporized because of new regulations banning fire-retardant baby clothes in America. It turned out that antimony trioxide, a product of stibnite ore with a history of profitable selling for anywhere between $600 and $7,200 a metric ton, was a carcinogenic material. In between unwrapping themselves from the ten-foot velvet bullcrackers strung around their bodies by the dancing girls, the traders pressed Busch on what he thought would be the next profitable metal. Busch said cadmium, another highly toxic metal removed from zinc ore with sulphuric acid and used to make polyvinyl chloride stabilizers and sprinkler systems.

"We were shit-faced drunk when we walked out of Miranda's," recalled one of the traders. "We got into someone's car and took a wrong turn down Carnaby Street, which is a pedestrian zone. People were yelling at us through the window and pounding the car with their fists, but the only thing we could hear was how much money we were going to make after pushing cadmium above its all-time high price of $5 a pound."

Before noon Tuesday Busch began unloading hundreds of tons of cadmium to the traders he had frolicked with the night before at Miranda's. By the time New York opened, every trader with a telephone was looking for cadmium. And the quantities they were asking for were staggering. Cadmium was traditionally offered in lots of sticks or ingots and sold in quantities no bigger than 5 tons, but now traders were pleading with Busch for shipments of 50 to 100 tons.

"Klaus, what's your price for cadmium?"

"I'm a buyer at three and seller at four if I have it."

"I'll buy 100 tons."

"Booked!"

"Klaus: I want another 50 tons!"

"Booked!"

"I thought you didn't have that much left?!"

"Found some more."

"Give me another ten tons!"

"Booked!"

The cadmium market collapsed Friday morning. The traders who had reveled with Busch at Miranda's started calling each other. Word was that traders everywhere were buying cadmium, but their industrial customers had plenty of the minor metal stockpiled and were loath to purchase more since the Busch-inspired frenzy had spiraled the price beyond reality. Five of the traders who had taken a bath on cadmium decided to meet at Langan's Brasserie on Stratton Street, where they pledged to drown their sorrows in wine and line their mucous membranes with cocaine. "After the fourth or fifth or sixth bottle of wine, it was decided that we had had enough of the metal business and that we'd meet at Langan's every Friday for the Klaus Busch Memorial Lunch," said one of the group's founders. "It was a great excuse for getting irresponsibly wasted like we did before we all became executive assholes."

But for the Marc Rich traders in attendance, the Heavy Metal Kids and their weekly Klaus Busch Memorial Lunch was a much-needed decompression chamber to relieve the ever-increasing agony of working in Rich's London office. Though the Kids resulted from the spontaneous combustion endemic to the commodity trading world, they were antithetical to the Marc Rich style of business, a fact that made the lunch all the more fun, prompting the Rich Kids to gladly foot the $200 to $300 bills with a laugh. "We were a small group of competitors who actually managed to find real friendship," said one of the two original Heavy Metal Kids who came from Marc Rich. "I guess you could say we were a bridge club for old hippies."

Membership in the Heavy Metal Kids is informal and open to anyone in the business. Within a year there were over twenty Heavy Metal Kids. Many of them traveled together, trading metals or attending industry conferences sponsored by *Metal Bulletin* around the world, from small industrial villages to cities starting with New York, Düsseldorf and Paris. The Kids were the party kings, and whenever a conference began to get boring, they were found rolling fat joints of marijuana and snorting the best cocaine money could buy off mirrors they had unscrewed from their hotel suite walls. The preferred drink was a vodka martini dry as sand, followed by steaks ordered so rare that chefs were required to "hit a cow over the head and light a match." In New York the bar was the Hudson Bay Inn on Second Avenue, a place popular with many Wall Street commodity brokers and always buzzing with the latest hot market gossip. Düsseldorf's contribution was Sam's West, an expensive drinking club where the Kids liked to loosen up before betting who could pull the youngest whore in the red light district. Party favors—which could run over $1,000 a night depending on how much cocaine was available—were put on the expense account.

More than any other event on the trading calendar, the Heavy Metal Kids look forward to the annual London Metal Exchange Dinner held every October in London's Grosvenor House. The LME Dinner is a dusk-to-dawn party in dozens of well-stocked hospitality suites rented for the evening by the corporations controlling the production, trading and consumption of the Earth's mineral wealth. Dinner begins promptly at 8 o'clock in the Great Room, a huge ice rink converted after World War Two into Europe's largest dining room.

The actions that yearly take place in the Grosvenor House suites are the evening's special scenes. Alongside corporate directors, Third World potentates and slickly dressed waiters passing drinks from silver trays are the Heavy Metal Kids. Trying to strike up conversations with the heads of major metal concerns, the Kids display the latest innovative uses for metal and have, on occasion, carried folding chrome Belgian trench knives in their pockets and worn sap gloves lined with eight ounces of evenly distributed lead powder. The evening never fails to get wild, forcing legitimate hotel guests either to bolt themselves behind closed doors or complain to the front desk about the rhythmical roar cascading through the hallways. Pranksters pile furniture into corners; entire floors are transformed into hospitality suites, a wilderness of fast-flowing bars populated by some of the industrial world's wealthiest and most powerful men, now reveling like Moose Lodgers and stiffer than steel girders. "The hotel has only four elevators, each with a maximum capacity of ten people," said a Heavy Metal Kid in a deadpan description of the social graces required to attend the LME dinner. "Traders must avoid the other players whom they have cheated, lied to or otherwise upset during the previous twelve months. It's important to institute polite conversations with dozens of people without revealing that you have completely forgotten their names."

The Grosvenor House staff, accustomed to the yearly dinner and all-night cocktail party, handle the behavior with true Tory breeding. Over the years they have tamed Communist-bloc executives who flashed fat rolls of dollars in front of any woman with the tenacity to remain in the open after midnight and calmly defused the Heavy Metal Kid from South Africa who earned his stripes by trying, unsuccessfully, to drive a truck into the hotel lobby.

The Kids consider the voyage to the autumn Guangchou Fair in China to be their clubhouse road trip, akin to a sailor's first crossing the equator. The fair trip is in late October, and the Kids depart London first class on board the Cathay Pacific flight from Gatwick to Bahrain to Hong Kong on the first Monday after the LME dinner. Telexes have been sent to the Peninsula Hotel with instructions that one of the hotel's green Rolls-Royces is to be waiting to whisk each trader individually into the city. Before going into China to buy raw ore and milled metal, the traders spend a few days at the Peninsula, meeting with their Southeast Asian agents to discover the latest news from inside the China National Metals and Minerals Import and Export Corporation (the largest of China's metal enterprises), the Non-Ferrous Metals Industrial Corporation and the Silver River—a Hong Kong hand-job parlor that one of the Kids named his Panamanian corporation after because the place took its name from a metal.

China and the whole Pacific Basin are important to the future of the commodity business. It's a vigorous area with huge populations, fast growth and an enormous appetite for making deals. In 1983, for instance, the United States traded more with Pacific countries than with its European allies. Though China had a mere $20 billion in hard currency reserves and a long way to go economically before catching up with its offshore neighbors, metal traders knew that the country's economy was profoundly dependent on exporting its mineral wealth in exchange for the Western currency required to build the economy. The flight into China is CAAC 304, leaving Hong Kong at 11:55 A.M. and arriving in Guangchou twenty-eight minutes later. Ground transportation to the Dung Fang Hotel, an ancient palace that was once a Mandarin playground, comes in the form of an air-conditioned cab or motorcycle sidecar, luggage piled atop the knees. "Go into the Dung Fang with a good supply of aerosol mace because the rats there are the size of Great Dane pups," said one of the Kids. "If any of the Chinese take you into downtown Guangchou for lunch be prepared to enjoy bat casserole and these ugly-looking sea slugs that stare back at you from soup."

The business of the Guangchou Fair takes place outside the Dung Fang, in a gigantic exposition hall festooned with flowers across a street filled with bell-jingling bicycle riders whom traders must dodge to avoid getting ground into the pavement. But life in Guangchou is easier than in the rest of China, making the city a genuinely different place to conduct business. Foreigners can telephone for appointments here, while in other cities they need permits in triplicate from the local Foreign Affairs Bureau before meetings can be arranged. The advantages of a liberal system are abundant: Guangchou generates over 10 percent of China's foreign exchange earnings and has become a required stop for any Westerner who wants to initiate business with the Chinese.

Guangchou's heat is sweltering, and the entire town is covered with a monotonous cloud of faintly luminous dust exuded by the industrial mills encircling the provincial capital. The atmosphere dictates the Chinese business dress code to be informal, but like everything in the trading world there is a price to be paid. "It's very difficult to have any respect for a Chinese corporate head who's wearing sandals, no socks and has the worst pedicure since Cro-Magnon man," observed a five-fair veteran visiting Guangchou to help the Chinese open

165

gold mines that could produce 45 metric tons of gold a year, making China the world's fourth-largest gold producer. Individual meetings are carried out in conference rooms located next to the exhibits of individual Chinese firms that have come to Guangchou to sell their products to the West for hard currency.

The moment a trader arrives in the conference room, he is given a cup of tepid jasmine tea with which to clear his throat. A uniformed waitress, whose only job is to refill the cup, stands behind the trader. During bargaining it's considered bad manners not to drink the tea continually, a process that demands strong kidneys of the visitor, because it's also frowned upon to leave a business conference to use the bathroom. Above each table is a large fan that swirls a wet wood-smelling fog of poorly grown Chinese tobacco throughout the room. Heavy spittoons filled with cigarette butts and cold tea ring the table. The negotiating pace is slow. It's rendered ever more tiring by the laborious translation process and the sheets of detailed ore specifications and gradings that must be analyzed for compatibility with Western mills. Perhaps unconsciously, a trader will spend hours listening impassively to the Chinese merchants pitch items in which he has no interest whatsoever just to develop a rapport with his hosts. Traders often lug out two airline pilot briefcases laden with metal samples presented to them as gifts at the conclusion of each meeting. It's impolite in China to refuse any gift; the guest is compelled to carry home two-pound chunks of ore and packets of powdered wolfram that make a trader's briefcase heavier than Klondike provision sacks.

"You must have the nerve to make deals quickly at a Guangchou Fair," an agent from Fidelity Mercantile explained during a fifteen-course banquet in celebration of a tungsten deal. "If you have the nerve and the money to conclude a deal, you can make an absolute fortune." In this context one metal man spent four days conducting some side action, trying to convince a representative from China's governing State Council that he should construct a tourist lodge on the site of an extant hunting reserve in Heilungkiang Province where foreigners could stay after shooting deer, lynx, bear and wild boar. Metal traders who have worked the Chinese coast for years say that the ultimate China deal is to purchase metal from a corporation in one province in the morning and then sell it to another province's metal firm in the afternoon. A Guangchou Fair legend says that this unique back-to-back deal has been accomplished only once, over "Nice Pasteries" in the Chun Hui coffee shop at the Dung Fang in the spring of 1984. Another story in the lore of the Heavy Metal Kids involved a trader from Associated Metals who was so bored that he bet a trader from Bomar Resources $1,000 to jump into the Dung Fang fountain to see if there were any goldfish alive underneath the coating of green slime. "There were goldfish alive down there," said the trader who lost the bet. "I couldn't believe it."

After spending two nonstop weeks of dealing amid the bugs and steam of Guangchou, Western traders return to the Peninsula to decompress before flying home or heading off to sell scrap metal to steel mills on Taiwan. The Heavy Metal Kids have a standing competition to find the most expensive prostitute on the Nationalist Chinese island nation. The current record is $500, the cost of a sex-filled evening that features monkey brains eaten in skull to enhance a patron's sexual desires. "By the time I left I was so wasted that I forgot the name of the place," said the trader, a thirty-six-year-old German who was first taken there while working in Tokyo in 1974. "No one will ever beat the record."

The Heavy Metal Kids made money just as well as they spent it. In early 1978 one of their number found himself in Zaire's Shaba Province, the location of about 65 percent of the world's cobalt production. He heard rumblings that a rebel army was preparing to invade, a move that would drive away most of the skilled white engineers who mined the cobalt, thus stimulating the free-market price. Upon his return to

167

London the Kid stockpiled as much cobalt as he could find and waited patiently. The rebels crossed into Shaba later that fall, kicking cobalt prices up from $5 to $40 a pound within the space of two months.

Bismuth—a chalky by-product of lead or zinc manufacture—was a golden nugget for the Heavy Metal Kid known fondly as the "French Fart King." This trader knew that the consumption of bismuth was subject to large price fluctuations because of its misuse as a suppository. Bismuth had a reputation for being the most volatile metal to trade; the reason was France, a country whose rectums consumed nearly 1,259 metric tons of bismuth (one-third of the world's production) to relieve indigestion in 1974. The Fart King, an English trader who sold the most bismuth to the French pharmaceutical industry, heard that the government was going to change bismuth's classification from over-the-counter drug to prescription remedy in the wake of complaints by medical authorities that too many Frenchmen were dying from the effects of inserting too much bismuth up their alimentary canals. Late in 1974 the King floated a rumor that he needed cash and began selling warehouses of bismuth to other traders. Everyone thought they had made a killing off the King's misfortune, but soon enough (by bismuth standards) the market had collapsed. By the middle of 1977 French consumption had fallen to 644 tons a year and by 1978 to only 346 tons. Bismuth's plunge was a direct result of the French population's overdosing on the metal. The Fart King, then a thirty-year-old trader, personified the finest traditions of the Heavy Metal Kids.

The most popular of all the Kids was Robbie Lichtenstern, Marc Rich's brash aluminum chief whose thirst for life best exemplified the waggish spirit of the group. Lichtenstern emerged from three generations of Dutch-Jewish traders; his father, Heinz, risked his own life to help smuggle fellow trader Meno Lissauer and his family out of Europe to avoid the concentration camps.

168

The Lichtenstern family was living in Amsterdam when war broke out in Europe. In 1940 Heinz, then a senior executive of the Lissauer Group, participated in a plan to pay off a Reich commissioner in gold and carry the Lissauers from Holland to Spain in a railroad car that had been secured through a phony letter of credit. Arriving in Spain the Lissauer family was smuggled out of the country with the help of a man called Tannenbaum, the local Lissauer Group trader.

Required to wear the Star of David and risking sterilization by Reich doctors authorized to neuter Dutch Jews, the Lichtensterns remained in Amsterdam until the autumn of 1943, when they were rounded up and deported via the Westerbrook transit station to the Theresienstadt concentration camp in Czechoslovakia. Theresienstadt, an old Bohemian fortress town, was Hitler's Potemkin village, a deadly film set for many prominent Jews whose disappearance might prove embarrassing to the Reich. The village was also a way station to the death camps, and according to the transit rota, the Lichtensterns were scheduled to leave the week of May 8, 1945—the week of Robbie's seventh birthday and the Allies' liberation of the camp. "What I remember of it was hell," Robbie Lichtenstern recalled three decades later in his clipped continental accent. "We lived off the orange peels the guards threw into the garbage." That horrible experience revealed itself in later life by his refusal to use the same towel twice, to dine only at the world's finest restaurants and always to champion the underdog.

After liberation the Lichtensterns sailed to Brazil, where Robbie became fluent in Portuguese, German, Dutch, French and English. The family moved to America in the mid-fifties. Heinz Lichtenstern went to work trading out of the Lissauer Group's offices in Manhattan while Robbie spent his teenage years going to school in the morning and stealing cars at night, a "hobby" that landed him in reform school by the time he was sixteen years old. As a young man Robbie rebeled against all attempts at discipline; he hated the metal business, pre-

169

ferring to spend his days wagering at backgammon. Finally, under pressure from his father and constant reminders from family friends that the Lichtenstern birth rite dictated he become a metal trader, he acquiesced and accepted a job arranged by his father making little more than $200 a week working for the Lissauer Group.

Robbie Lichtenstern became a great metal trader because he loved gambling; he also ran up nearly $30,000 worth of gaming debts while a young trader in London. It was impossible to pay off his gaming house creditors on a $200-a-week salary, so Robbie went to his father for help. Heinz Lichtenstern believed that his son's life would come together once he married and told his son that he would float him a five-year loan if he settled down into a normal lifestyle. Although he never repaid his father or settled into a conventional lifestyle, Robbie did marry, and went on to develop what many traders believed to be the finest trading mind in the profession, honing his prodigious talents as a strategic metals trader in Europe, the Far East and South America.

Lichtenstern was one of the first traders outside Philipp Brothers to join ranks with Marc Rich in 1974. He established himself quickly as the firm's top trader and was gladly welcomed by Rich's Inner Circle. But there was more to Robbie Lichtenstern than his vivid trading skills. He was a passionate man, interested in people, who vehemently avoided any suggestion of betraying a friendship for the sake of a deal. "Robbie never screwed anyone on a deal," a trader for Derek Raphael explained. "Robbie knew how to make money, but never at the cost of a friendship."

Robbie Lichtenstern enjoyed overindulgence and never ceased to stretch the limits of his Bohemian world. He voiced no qualms about renting women for Rich customers visiting London, spending—by his own account—some $25,000 a year on call girls, many of whom became his friends outside the bedroom. He smoked marijuana for the first time in the mid-seventies while living in a flat on Portman Square in London.

170

A trader he worked with had just returned from a business trip to Africa bearing a wrapped banana leaf that had been stuffed with an extremely potent Zimbabwean grass and buried underground for three months, a procedure designed to heighten the ferocity of the weed to psychedelic levels. Watching the trader chip tiny chunks of African cannabis from the solidified banana leaf with a kitchen knife, Lichtenstern became worried that he might do something awful while under the drug's influence and decided to tie pillows to all the living room furniture to avoid injury if "reefer madness" set in. "I warned Robbie to take only one small hit," the trader said, recalling the evening. "Robbie wouldn't listen. He sucked up three large tokes and complained that he didn't feel anything. Then he vomited all over his French poodle."

Lichtenstern passed out cold on the sofa, but the first thing he asked for on regaining consciousness a few hours later was where he could get his hands on a two-ton container of Zimbabwean banana grass. He soon developed a sophisticated taste for recreational drugs, particularly exotic marijuanas and Peruvian cocaine. He toted his stash around the world in a leather briefcase, securing his five Thai sticks in pen loops. (Thai sticks are a powerful Asian-grown marijuana entwined securely around a 5-inch bamboo sliver.) On a shopping trip to a luggage store, he had a salesman customize a case so that it could hold cocaine with more fiendish economy. "Robbie like to say that his briefcases were designed to 'carry more dope than documents,' " a London trader recalled.

Robbie Lichtenstern tested taboos. Driving recklessly through the streets of Rio de Janeiro with another Marc Rich trader and two women one evening in 1979, Lichtenstern heard the blare of a police siren catching up with his rented car. Before pulling over to the curb, he handed a vial of cocaine to the women sitting next to him, assuring them that he would take care of everything if their party was busted. The police discovered the stash and took the passengers to a jail. The women were nervous—drug laws in Brazil are harsh—but Lichten-

171

stern merely telephoned a minister in the military government
who had helped him buy Brazilian metals. Since Lichtenstern
was an important source of the American dollars needed so
desperately to help pay off Brazil's foreign debt—the world's
biggest—everyone was released. No questions asked.

Drugs were used by traders in the Marc Rich organization
to blunt the stress of twenty-four-hour days on the theory that
simple deceleration would lighten the pain. But it was a different sort of tension that Lichtenstern began to speak of
privately to intimates in 1983. "Robbie complained that selling your soul to Marc was a condition of the contract," a trader
who worked closely with Lichtenstern remembered. "He
wanted a way out."

"It got to the point where Robbie felt there was too much
pressure and it wasn't worth it anymore," said Robbie's adopted
brother, Warner Kolb. "He talked about that quite a lot."

Added one of Rich's shareholders: "It was the oil money
that made everybody crazy. There was so much money that
Marc, Robbie, everybody in the firm lost touch with reality."

What was happening to the lives of Marc Rich traders was
not a problem of simple overindulgence. It was about balance,
about karma, about people who became inflated and vulnerable from breaking all the rules, not anticipating that they
themselves could be broken by them. Robbie Lichtenstern—
the lovable scoundrel who became the greatest trader at Marc
Rich and the "guiding spirit" of its ambitious rank and file—
was just coming to understand the ubiquitous danger of the
Marc Rich organization when he died abruptly in the intensive
care unit of a Zurich hospital on June 30, 1984.

The coroner said Lichtenstern was killed by a cerebral hem-
orrhage that had hit him in a hotel room three days earlier,
adding that if he had survived, he would have been blind in
the right eye, his body frozen in paralysis.

He had just turned forty-six years old.

Two London call girls—on whom Lichtenstern had spent
more love than money—stood alone outside the brick pavilion

of the Reformed Jewish Cemetery in London and let the faint July breeze dry their tears. The rabbi revealed that Robbie had told her a few months before that he would not lead a long life. She added during the eulogy that "Robbie was high on life." One of the Heavy Metal Kids pushed his tears away with a clenched fist and strained to chuckle that "Robbie was high on everything." The Pound Lane gravedigger leaned against his shovel and said that the size of the grave was extraordinary to accommodate the casket's girth: Robbie Lichtenstern always disliked dieting.

"Robbie was running too fast," said another Kid, unable to come to grips with the passing of his pal. "He'd been losing it the past few months, screwing up deals . . . he didn't care. I think he wanted out . . . no one quits Marc Rich."

In life Robbie Lichtenstern was the architect of Marc Rich's fabulously profitable bauxite cartel, the trader who made his boss the world's most powerful broker of aluminum, a fact evidenced by the flowers and written condolence sent by Edward Seaga, prime minister of Jamaica.

Denise Rich attended the funeral, escorting Robbie's widow, Angela, and their two children out of the chapel. The doges of the international commodity industry were at the Fourth of July funeral too—nearly 300 of them, coming in limousines and a convoy of thirty black London cabs.

"Bastards!" one of the Heavy Metal Kids snapped when he saw Felix Posen, manager of Rich's London office, begin talking about the future of the company's aluminum book with a member of the Inner Circle. "Fuckers! It's another fucking business meeting."

It seemed that the only two people in the commodity business who failed to appear at the Pound Lane cemetery were Marc Rich and his sidekick, Pinky Green. Oddly, they were not conspicuous in their absence, except to the man from the United States Justice Department who crouched uncomfortably near a gravestone, photographing the mourners. Along with the nervous Scotland Yard inspector beside an arbor, only the man holding the camera believed Rich and Green might come to lament the company's top trader with the rest of their fraternity.

Marc Rich and Pinky Green were in Zug and had no intention of braving its border to pay final tribute, even with their new non-American passports. They were not absent because of embarrassment at publicly mourning a man to whose death the company's inertia had contributed. The pair had buried traders before. The situation was more delicate. Rich and Green were wanted men, on the lam from a fifty-one-count indictment accusing them of racketeering, mail and wire fraud, tax evasion, conspiracy, price fixing and possible charges of treason stemming from the violation of a trade ban with the Ayatollah Ruhollah Khomeini.

They had been charged, in great part, under the Racketeer Influenced and Corrupt Organization (RICO) statutes—laws that were enacted specifically to handcuff major dope dealers and businessmen like Al Capone. All in all, the burial of Robbie Lichtenstern was reminiscent of a Cosa Nostra funeral, with mourners who would all make splendid witnesses for the prosecution.

CHAPTER 15

"Confusion is a word we have invented for an order which is not understood."

HENRY MILLER, *Tropic of Cancer*

A S THE OLD Panhandle oil fields of scrub brush and shit-kickers gave way to the modern world—designer mesquite and $1,800 alligator boots—the business of oil, too, changed. Oil lost its frontier luster after the Arab embargo. It became a business of gluts and deficits, of write-downs and interest rates, all revolving around a legacy of depletion allowances and scumbled regulations interpreted by expensive lawyers and specialized accountants. The only real action was left to the crooks.

There were six oil price disruptions during the seventies, and each one of them was invigorated by government regulations to control the price and production of American oil. Between 1973 and 1981 fumbling federal laws were enacted to create specific classifications for American oil, with specific prices assigned legally to each classification. These laws, which centered on how long an oil well had been producing prior to the regulations, were created ostensibly to relieve the financial burden high oil prices were placing on the American consumer. The system was an expensive farce.

There were three oil groups: old, new and stripper. So-called old oil was crude being pumped at or below a 1972 production level. The new federal laws required "old" oil to be sold cheapest of the three. "New" oil was crude from wells opened since 1973 or crude from wells producing in excess of 1973 levels; it could be sold at a higher price. The highest-priced oil was stripper oil—crude taken from wells pumping an average of less than ten barrels a day. Stripper oil sold for the highest price, being the only one free from price regulation.

The regulations were administered by the Department of Energy, but bureaucratic bungling allowed unscrupulous traders the opportunity to take illegal, short-term profits by simply passing slips of paper through a series of bogus oil brokers. The procedure was known within the industry as "flipping the price," or by its more popular term, "daisy chaining."

Each reseller added a markup of 25 cents to $1 a barrel, then sold the oil to the next link in the daisy chain. Somewhere along the chain, a broker illegally relabeled the old oil as new or stripper oil, and paid himself a huge markup for his risk. Once this oil reached the hands of the final broker, it was disposed of at whatever price the market would bear.

Since old oil was forced to sell at around $6 a barrel, dealers reclassified old as new, then offered customers crude petroleum that would legally sell at $6 a barrel for anywhere from $25 to $40 a barrel.

American oil companies buy, sell and refine oil into gasoline and other petrochemical products. The refineries are engineered to process certain grades of oil, some of which must be bought from outside the United States; thus, a certain amount of foreign oil is needed regularly. If foreign oil can be bought cheaply and an oil company already has a sufficient supply of that grade, it will be glad to buy and resell it at a profit. In any case it has no choice but to sell its domestic oil to a domestic or foreign refinery that can process those grades. Therefore a major American oil company must both buy and sell oil.

This circumstance, the context of the oil crisis and the new federal regulations, opened a door as large as a bank vault for the crooks. The basic scam was this: A trader bought OPEC oil, for example, at a higher price than the official OPEC price (there was an oil drought under way) but lower than the true market price, i.e., spot prices. This satisfied the nationalized foreign oil companies and, when the trader sold it to an American firm at a price still under spot, pleased the refiner. In exchange the American oil company would sell domestic old oil—the $6-a-barrel variety that it wanted to dump—back to the trader at a slight discount (say, $5 a barrel) so the trader could pipe it into a daisy chain, where it would be fraudulently relabeled and shot out the other end at a price close to spot (say, $35).

By 1978 the Department of Energy was unable to account for over 200,000 barrels of old oil that was vanishing from the government accounting system each day. This phenomenal figure—which between 1973 and 1981 added up to 400 million barrels of old oil—was reached by comparing the amount of old oil bought at the wellhead with the amount of old oil that arrived at a refinery. At a congressional hearing investigating the malfeasance and indifference of the Department of Energy in regard to daisy chaining, Michigan Congressman John Conyers, chairman of the Subcommittee on Crime, asked a federal prosecutor familiar with the scam to estimate how much of the American dollar paid at the gas pump was traceable to profits from daisy chaining. The witness, attorney Marvin Rudnick, said, "You can make an estimate that two-thirds of the 92.9 cents I paid for gas in Tampa last week could be the subject of that type of crime." Between 1974 and 1978 consumers had been cheated out of at least $2 billion. Something was out of whack.

Energy Department auditors cottoned on to what was happening in 1980. They figured out that a new clique of traders was discounting foreign oil to the major oil companies in return for old oil which the traders marked as new oil to be sold at the highest possible price. The oil companies, meanwhile, were the cooperative producers who gave the appearance of doing nothing illegal; they were just selling their domestic production in accordance with government guidelines. And all the bureaucrats saw at first was a chaos of paper, unaware that one man's confusion is another man's devious system.

The light eventually shed on the conspiracy was foggy, at best. Before the Arab oil embargo, there were only twelve oil resellers in the United States. By 1978 there were 500 companies pimping old, new and stripper oil. Many of these outfits reclassified documents of origin and then resold the oil for whatever refineries were willing to pay. Since there were long lines of gas station customers prepared to pay any price to fill their tanks, refiners were willing to shell out a hell of a lot. The Department of Energy decided to slap a limit of 20 cents profit per barrel of resold oil, a directive that merely caused the daisy chainers to hide their profits, because they continued to sell their oil at the highest possible price.

David Ratliff and John Troland were two Texas oil laundrymen who were wringing huge profits out of the daisy chain. In 1979 they formed West Texas Marketing, an Abilene company that bought and then resold domestic crude to whoever knocked on their office door. One of the Texans' first visitors was Marc Rich, who had just been initiated into the rituals of the modern American oil business through a joint venture with Denver oilman Marvin Davis, his partner in Twentieth Century-Fox, to purchase wells in Louisiana and Oklahoma. "The company was thriving at the time, and we had no need to make money by buying domestic wells or daisy chaining oil," one of Rich's senior oil traders explained. "But Marc and Pinky saw others making a fortune out of daisy chaining and decided that they'd be able to get away with it.

"Pinky really instigated the idea. He wanted to muscle in on the domestic oil business and convinced Marc that we could do it. We had recently finished an oil deal with South Africa that screwed them out of an extra $400 million on about three or four shipments. Marc said the South Africans didn't complain, so why should anyone else?"

Troland and Ratliff were Rich's kind of folks—unethical and greedy. They also needed help in financing West Texas Marketing through a bank that would be more understanding of the particular needs of trading on a tightrope. Rich introduced them to Cie Financière de Paris et des Pays-Bas, the huge French bank that financed and grew fat off many of Rich's Third World commodity deals. "Troland and Ratliff came in for a meeting," recalled a senior Rich executive. "Marc and Pinky listened because there was a deal to be made. About one-fifth of our business was in the United States, and Marc saw West Texas Marketing as another way to increase our presence."

Rich and Green also arranged in 1979 for Arco to sell 18 million barrels of old Alaskan oil to a bogus Listo Petroleum, a Houston-based daisy chain tended by Clyde Meltzer. That oil was reportedly spun around as many as sixteen separate subcompanies; Arco had gladly piped their oil to Listo in return for Rich's supplying Arco's refineries with hard-to-get foreign crude.

The next step in the daisy chain was for Rich's Swiss company to resell the relabeled oil back to Listo or out to West Texas Marketing at the current market price. The buyers then sold the oil to one of Rich's secret Panamanian companies at a loss. The amount lost was recaptured when Rich's Panamanian company immediately sold the undervalued oil at the full market price to an outsider in what would be the final transaction in the daisy chain. The profits from these deals— that is, the amount "lost" and recaptured in the last two moves—were deposited in offshore accounts owned by secret corporations controlled by the principal links in the daisy chain sequence. It was a precise paper scam: While the oil never physically moved anywhere, the money always clustered outside the country.

By 1980 West Texas Marketing was generating over $2

billion a year on oil. Their average daily volume was 300,000 barrels, much of it coming directly from Arco. Marc Rich International was responsible for some 10 percent of West Texas Marketing's sales and was angling for more by Christmas. Troland and Ratliff were enormously pleased: They paid themselves $750,000 apiece for 1980 and celebrated their good fortune by throwing a Christmas party for their employees and business friends. Learjets whisked all over the country to fly the company's customers to the Abilene Country Club. Expensive gifts and envelopes stuffed with year-end bonuses were passed around like so many Cheez Doodles. Troland, the chairman of West Texas Marketing, presented himself a prickly ostrich-skin jacket and matching boots; Ratliff decided on a dune buggy. Marc Rich went skiing in St. Moritz.

The gravy train derailed in March 1981 when Justice Department attorneys, investigating forty-seven separate cases of daisy chaining worth over $79 million, discovered that Troland and Ratliff were involved in a 1979 con (unrelated to Rich) to recertify controlled domestic oil. The high-flying Texans were shot down and sentenced to fourteen months in a federal prison camp in Big Spring, Texas. But a few days before they were to begin serving soft time, Troland met Rich in Manhattan to divvy up their loot. There was much confusion over just how much cash was in the Rich–West Texas Marketing treasure chest of illegal deals. Rich claimed that some of the records were missing; others had stains covering important figures; many critical details had disappeared all together. Rich and Troland argued, some say violently. There was only a few million dollars in the pot, much less than Troland had been led to believe. Arrangements were made to split the cash offshore. Troland went to prison an angry man.

Troland and Ratliff were flown to Washington in May 1981 to be interrogated further by Justice Department attorneys on what they knew of other daisy chaining scams. A few weeks after their visit to Washington, federal marshals accompanied them to Houston, where they were questioned by Sandy Weinberg, a thirty-year-old federal prosecutor from the United States Southern District Court of New York. Weinberg asked the two men if West Texas Marketing had ever helped another company avoid paying taxes by handling money for them. Troland and Ratliff, hoping for a deal, said "Marc Rich." Sandy Weinberg had never heard the name.

PART IV
THERE WAS
A CROOKED MAN

CHAPTER 16

There was a crooked man, and he went a crooked mile,
He found a crooked sixpence beside a crooked stile;
He bought a crooked cat, which caught a crooked mouse,
And they all lived together in a little crooked house.

MOTHER GOOSE

O N THE FLIGHT back from Houston to La Guardia Airport, Sandy Weinberg pondered what he had heard in the Houston hotel room a few hours earlier. He had yet to see any documents, but he knew the sheer dollar value of Rich's daisy chain would make any litigation against him galactic in scope. Weinberg had an impressive trophy case of successful white-collar criminal prosecutions. He had been with the Justice Department for only five years but had already handled twenty-five criminal cases, more than any other prosecutor in the New York office. A Tennessee hills boy with a long Fess Parker drawl, he was responsible for successfully prosecuting the largest Medicare fraud in history, a decision that sent a doctor to prison for ten years and collected fines of $800,000. He had also helped sanitize the Agency for International Development, cleaning up a situation in which freight shippers were overcharging the agency $50 million to forward food and medical supplies to Bangladesh. "The Rich case would be different," Weinberg thought as his plane landed in Queens. "I'm really going to have to start from absolute scratch."

Sandy Weinberg started drafting a prosecution team in the fall of 1981. It would come to include agents from the Federal Bureau of Investigation, the Treasury Department, the Customs Service and the State Department. At its core were federal attorneys Jane Parver, Martin Auerbach and Larry Pedowitz. The elder statesman of the squad was Special Agent #633, Morty Dick, a fifty-year-old Brooklyn Law School alumnus with a .38 caliber snub nose clipped to his belt. Dick's Bowery Boy face had seen every hustle and dodge ever invented. He even had a few of his own. His last assignment effectively shattered a movie tax shelter fraud by proving a 108-count federal indictment. "The trick to this case," he told Weinberg, "is to take the complications and make them simple." Putting Dick's advice into action came to be a long, tedious and ridiculous task.

Weinberg's team had no real idea of what they might find. The only certainty was that its lawyers were anathemas to Marc Rich's trading world. This was particularly true of Sandy Weinberg, an individual whose life was magnetically opposed to the man he was preparing to tangle with. Sandy Weinberg's real name was Morris Weinberg, Jr., but his mother, a Tennessee Baptist who married a New York Jew, convinced the family that their son should be called Sandy. Sandy's brother was a Rhodes Scholar who changed his name to Keda Sari Weinberg after joining a Buddhist ashram in England.

Sandy Weinberg was schooled during the Tet Offensive and the Watergate Summer, graduating with an understanding that criminals need not look like guest stars on *Kojak* to be sent to jail. He had experienced an age that gave him a special reason for going after men like Marc Rich, the kind of crooks whose money, power and political clout obviated any need to holster guns underneath their coats. Weinberg didn't arrive at the Foley Square courthouse in a chauffeur-driven Mercedes-Benz; he came by subway and walked around the bums huddling for warmth over the steam grates in front of his office. He wasn't a zealot for social justice, but he had a unique affinity for the little guy; moreover he knew that Marc Rich was ripping off the system. And that was against the law.

In the beginning of 1982 a federal grand jury issued subpoenas to John Piskora, Greg Garrick, Dick Mantel, Clyde Meltzer, Robert Aronson, Jim Lancaster, John Harris and ten other executives working for Marc Rich International in New York City. At the top of this list was John Piskora, one of Rich's oil traders and the man who first introduced Rich and Green to Troland and Ratliff. Also served with federal subpoenas were Arco oil executives Bill Ariano, Frank Smith, Joe Wortman and Rus Osborne. By the time the grand jury concluded its investigation, it would have called fifty people to provide testimony.

Over the next few months Weinberg subpoenaed 200,000 pages of financial, traffic and telex records from Rich's New York office and convinced Mobil, Exxon and Shell to turn over further documents without issuing any court order. Weinberg had to navigate through a floor-to-ceiling maze of boxed documents to reach his desk.

Rich and Green remained in New York, conducting their business from the Piaget Building as if the government probe was of no importance. Their chief lawyer was Washington kingpin Edward Bennett Williams, who, thought Rich and Green, was being paid enough money to contain any problems that might arise out of the grand jury investigation. The only executives squirming were Rich's oil traders. "We knew that we were dead the first quarter of 1982," one of them explained. "No one else in the company cared because they had somehow come to believe that the Department of Energy regulations we were being accused of breaking were no longer in effect. What they failed to understand, or maybe didn't want to understand, was that the government was still enforcing the laws if you broke them while they were still in effect." Of course, they had probably done more than break a handful of ill-conceived Department of Energy regulations.

According to Rich insiders Pinky Green convinced his partner that the government would never indict them. "At first Marc wanted to try and negotiate a payoff, but Pinky talked him out of it," said one of Rich's senior European oil traders. "Pinky was really arrogant . . . treated the United States like a sleezy Nigerian oil minister. You know, let's out-deal these bastards; they're just like anyone else we deal with."

Sandy Weinberg had other ideas and incessantly recalled Rich employees for testimony in front of the grand jury, offering immunity if they divulged all. Many of the traders called had only a superficial understanding of the daisy chain, but to be offered immunity is to imply guilt. Not sure of what they might be guilty, most of them gladly accepted Weinberg's deal and handed the team detailed accounts of Rich's commodity empire.

Rich and Green grew worried. Although only privileged, ranking insiders had full knowledge of the corporation's global affairs, it was eminently clear that Weinberg had the subpoena power to construct an indictment that might force Rich publicly to reveal the full extent of his business operations. Edward Bennett Williams visited Weinberg and offered a $100 million settlement if he dropped the pending charges against Rich and Green to misdemeanors. Weinberg said no, telling Williams that "as long as we have Rich and Green, it's a case of people, not money." Weinberg's reaction to the offer floored Rich and Green: they thought everything had a price.

Weinberg, however, had the ammunition to shoot for something much bigger than any settlement money. Under grand jury questioning, Rich trader John Piskora revealed that he kept a personal log of oil transactions between Marc Rich International, West Texas Marketing, Listo Petroleum and Marc Rich AG—International's Swiss parent/protector. Rich, according to sources in his office, was stunned. He apparently had had no idea that Piskora was keeping a record, believing that all dangerous documentation had gone through the office paper shredder or been sent to the safety of Zug. Weinberg churned out more subpoenas, ordering Rich's Swiss company to deliver "any and all records, documents and other papers pertaining to any and all foreign and domestic crude oil transactions for the years 1980 and 1981."

An inescapable spectre of treachery was settling in over Rich's New York headquarters. Too many people were talking and Rich had to do something about it. He knew that Weinberg would subpoena any traders whom he fired. And if any of the traders who had already testified were dismissed, he would forfeit any opportunity to discover what they might have told Weinberg about the corporation's activities. It was essential that a facade be erected—make Weinberg believe that it was business as usual at Marc Rich.

But employees called in front of the grand jury—who had been ensured all the moral and financial support they might require—were beginning to be discriminated against by Rich and the rest of his Inner Circle. Fellow workers would avoid them in the hallways, and they were told not to attend meetings at which they had been scheduled to appear. "It all depended on how much money you made for him," said a witness who testified in front of the grand jury. "If you made a lot of money for him, you got a personal summons to visit his office to be told that everything was okay.

"If you were in a nonmoney-generating position, then you got the cold shoulder. Marc didn't want to know about you. You were treated like a piece of shit."

In April 1982 Marc Rich refused to comply with the grand jury's request to turn over documents being held in Zug. His lawyers argued that as a Swiss company, Marc Rich AG was immune from any United States court order. Rich's position ignited a year of intractable appeals and motions in front of Leonard B. Sand, a federal judge with a white beard and a striking resemblance to Walter Matthau. Rich used his vast cash reserves to pay the best lawyers money could buy—so many defense attorneys that finding enough table space to accommodate them all in Judge Sand's courtroom became serious business. Over the next two years Rich's legal staff

189

would grow to include the firms of Edward Bennett Williams; Proskauer, Rose, Goetz and Mendelsohn; Arnold and Porter; Curtis, Mallet-Prevost, Colt & Mosle; Kramer, Levin, Nessen, Kamin and Frankel; Milgrim, Thomajan, Jacobs and Lee; the Swiss law firms of Paul Stadlin, Hans Barth and Rudolf Moismann—as well as Boris Kostelanetz, the brother of composer André Kostelanetz; Peter Zimroth, the husband of actress Estelle Parsons, and Michael Tigar, an attorney who defended the Chicago Seven and the Seattle Eight. Back in Switzerland, Rich and Green were being referred to as the "Zug Two."

There was more cash than eloquence displayed during the seventeen motions, six appeals and 3 million documents argued in courtroom number 128. "Face it, Marc Rich is a golden tit," said one of Rich's lawyers, commenting on a story that any third-year law student could telephone Rich, say that he was interested in the case, and be sent a retainer for $25,000.

Rich treated his lawyers like bears dancing for their supper. The hearings were sloggy affairs designed by Rich to muddle, bedevil, flummox and take advantage of every legal loophole his cash could unearth. Whenever a particular legal issue became especially murky, requiring everyone in the courtroom to spend a week at the law library, Rich would change counsel so that the whole procedure could be repeated to stretch delays even further. At one twisted point in the hearing, Judge Sand looked down from his bench to see an entirely new set of defense lawyers trying to explain the issues of the day's hearing to yet another gaggle of new faces. "I will take a five-minute recess to enable counsel for Marc Rich incoming, outgoing, or whatever, to confer with each other."

At issue throughout the eighteen months of hearings was Article 273 of the Swiss Penal Code, a clever bit of legislation that supported Rich's contention that it would be "economic espionage" for his Swiss company to release the documents that Weinberg wanted to add to the government's collection. Weinberg argued that eleven of the traders employed by International in New York were actually working for AG in Switzerland, and that there was ample evidence provided by the grand jury that documents pertaining to Rich's activities in the United States were being hidden in Switzerland.

Judge Sand agreed. On September 15, 1982, he issued a contempt of court citation ordering Rich to deliver the documents or to start paying a fine of $50,000 per business day until they were delivered. Rich's lawyers flooded the court with appeals and the fine was shelved until May 1983, when the Second Circuit Court of Appeals ordered Rich to deliver a cashier's check for the full amount on a twice-weekly basis to the Federal Clerk of Courts.

Trying to circumvent the fine, Rich claimed that to comply with Judge Sand's order would be to violate Swiss law, but in a great fanfare of accommodation, he loudly urged a Swiss court to rule that Marc Rich AG must comply. Meanwhile, knowing full well that he was one of Zug's largest employers of Swiss nationals and a major source of cantonal tax revenue, Rich pressured officials in Berne to induce the court to rule against compliance on the grounds that, if he opened his books on business conducted abroad, then every American company with a Swiss doppelgänger could be forced to open its books.

The situation Rich created was a classic double bind: Which country's laws should be honored? The fallout from the dilemma stood to disrupt the entire, global marketplace. When the American hostages were locked in the embassy in Iran, President Carter froze all of Iran's assets in the United States and in the foreign branches of American banks. Although the host governments grudgingly complied, the action opened up an entirely fresh can of worms. What was to be done about Dresser Industries, an American company, if its European arm honored a deal to supply France with equipment with which to construct the Soviet-European natural gas pipeline? How was the Securities and Exchange Commission going to appeal a decision by Switzerland's highest court not to reveal the names of American citizens who conducted insider trading in connection with the $2.5 billion takeover of Santa Fe International by Kuwait Petroleum Corporation, because insider trading is not a crime in Switzerland? And what about the other grand jury sitting in St. Louis, investigating whether or not International Telephone and Telegraph tried to sell Iran $4.2 million worth of the bolts needed to join electrical wires, via fake bank accounts, false shipping labels and salesmen with Finnish and Swedish passports?

Defending the Swiss court's action in the Rich case in another appeal a few months later, the chief prosecutor of Zug wrote:

> The defendant trades largely (but not exclusively) in crude oil and crude oil products. It trades, as well as all trading firms, in and with countries which are from a political aspect extremely sensitive and which are partially involved with and against each other in political arguments and clashes (for instance, the Near East, South America, Africa, China, the states of the Eastern bloc). In addition, the trade goods, in particular crude oil and its products, but other raw materials in which the defendant trades, are of high political significance. It is not difficult to understand under these circumstances that especially governments or state-operated trading companies prefer to use intermediary trade (such as, for instance, through the petitioner) for trading with other countries. The reasons for this are many: especially the wish to keep the purchase and sales strategies for certain trade goods secret, to cover up contradictions between economic and political actions, or also only to avoid difficulties resulting from the import—export—or trade obstacles raised by individual states. A disclosure of such transactions and their details would have considerable and very disadvantageous consequences for all participants, and not only for the defendant but primarily also for those responsible in the individ-

ual countries who may be jeopardized, not excluding physical harm.

Sandy Weinberg started crawling walls. He told Judge Sand in open court that the whole thing was "ludicrous, contrived and concocted." Klaus Weber, the Swiss cantonal court judge who issued the injunction keeping Rich's documents in Zug, said: "I'm embarrassed by [my] decision."

The Swiss court's order was scandalous by American standards. Rich was represented in Switzerland by Rudolf Moismann, the chief prosecutor for Canton Zug, who was also a director of Marc Rich AG, as well as thirty-three other foreign firms registered in Zug. Peter Hess, Moismann's chief assistant, sat on twenty-six corporate boards and Zug police chief Urs Kohler was a member of another ten. Rich went beyond covering all the bases; he bought the ballpark.

Based on the decision of the Swiss court, Rich's American defense team went to the United States Supreme Court to ask that the $50,000-a-day fine be thrown out. The Supreme Court refused to hear the appeal. On June 29, 1983, Marc Rich was ordered to commence payment of $50,000 a day to protect documents that Sandy Weinberg called the "golden nuggets" to a successful prosecution. Although the fine was, in the words of a Rich trader, "Saturday night boogie money for Marc," Rich refused to pay. There were still a few more tricks he could use to confuse the man who was fashioning an indictment that could send him to jail for 325 years.

Sweating from a crowded subway commute down from Manhattan's East 77th Street station, Sandy Weinberg trudged into his office on St. Andrew's Plaza the morning of June 30, 1983, and knocked over a 23-inch-high stack of documents as he reached for his ringing telephone. He had yet to have his coffee and was not in the mood to deal with the noisy machine. Weinberg picked up the stained receiver, said "hello" and listened. The early morning silence of the seventh floor was broken when everybody in the office heard Sandy Weinberg scream, "He did what!!!"

On the evening of June 29, Marc Rich prepared a two-page, forty-line document that sold Marc Rich International to a new company called Clarendon Limited, a firm with the same fifty traders, twelve traffic managers, thirty-five finance executives, phone numbers and address as Marc Rich International. Even the company's board remained the same. Almost. There was one cosmetic change: Marc Rich and Pinky Green were no longer listed as directors. Willi Strothotte, the Inner Circle member who was installed as Clarendon's chief operating officer, asserted that "any charges arising against Clarendon would be strictly a matter of money," because there "aren't any personalities involved," despite the new company's bank credit being guaranteed by Marc Rich.

A fresh flock of lawyers representing Marc Rich's doppelgänger plodded into court a few days later to tell the judge that the new company was not liable to pay the $50,000-a-day fine. Judge Sand listened politely before exploding. He angrily called the scheme "a ploy to frustrate the implementation of the court's order." On July 17, 1984, he ordered Marc Rich AG to pay $500,000 of its outstanding fine and told Weinberg to freeze all of AG's assets in the United States. But since Marc Rich AG had sold its sole American asset—Marc Rich International—to Clarendon, Weinberg slapped restraining orders on companies that owed money to Marc Rich AG. Weinberg then blocked a whopping $55 million owed to Rich, on top of enforcing the daily fine. By the end of the year, the frozen assets would have grown to include $50 million worth of American oil wells controlled jointly by Marc Rich and Marvin Davis, Rich's Guam Oil and Refining Company, and $116 million worth of Twentieth Century-Fox voting stock.

"Imagine," Weinberg chuckled, "the United States government might end up owning Twentieth Century-Fox."

Rich's lawyers, now numbering over twenty, counterattacked on August 5. They promised to produce more documents and to make a $1.2 million down payment on the fines. They also said Rich would turn over the records of three of Rich's Panamanian companies—Liquin Resources, Highams Consultants and Rescor. The three Panamanian shells, Weinberg believed, contained meaty kernels of information pertaining to crude oil schemes from 1979 through 1981. Rich's posture of cooperation, however, was yet another stall. This time Weinberg was prepared.

On Tuesday night, August 9, 1983, Morty Dick's special agents, acting on a tip, radioed the Kennedy Airport tower and ordered controllers to stop Swissair flight #111 from taking off for Geneva and Zurich. They boarded the 747 and detained a female paralegal working for Rich's defense team who was attempting to leave the country with two steamer trunks full of the documents that Rich had promised to deliver to Weinberg.

The next day Sandy Weinberg requested that the court allow him to find out whom all the new lawyers in the courtroom were representing: He really wasn't sure. Whoever they were, they stood in front of Judge Sand and told him that the papers were being flown to Zug so that Marc Rich and Pinky Green, who had left Manhattan for Zug a few days earlier, could "review them in an attempt to speed up compliance with Your Honor's orders." Morty Dick left the courtroom to put stake-out teams on the Piaget Building.

Though Leonard Sand had the look of a Tombstone Territory judge ready to stretch the necks of Rich's lawyers from the nearest oak, there was a whole new series of legal complications that needed to be handled with extreme delicacy. Switzerland's ambassador to the United States, Anton Hegner, had personally delivered an official note of protest to the State Department over what Switzerland considered to be heavy-handed American prosecution methods. Zug's public prosecutor said that his friends were "being held as hostages" and that the American courts were involved in "economic intelligence gathering." Zug's finance director, Georg Stucky, complained that Marc Rich and Pinky Green were being "blackmailed" by the United States. Officials in Berne responded by sending Joseph Guttentag and Juerg Leutert to represent the Swiss government in the New York City courtroom as observers, often contributing to the proceedings.

"The central issue here," hectored Matthias Krafft, a Swiss government official in charge of international legal questions, "is that Marc Rich is a Swiss entity. You have a tendency to consider firms that are controlled by Americans but domiciled in Switzerland to be under United States jurisdiction."

"We have six large tax contributors who influence our financial budget," Zug Mayor Othmar Kamer reminded his citizens. "Marc Rich is one of them."

"The future of the Swiss system is on trial here," one of the lawyers representing Switzerland explained privately. "We do not want to lose Marc Rich and others like him. It would ruin Switzerland."

Not only had the Swiss government helped to defend Marc Rich and Pinky Green through the management of public opinion and by allowing government-paid lawyers to become de facto members of Rich's defense team, but now the Soviet Union was becoming involved in an official capacity. Rich was a big Soviet customer, greasing the state-controlled economy with millions in hard Western currencies in return for being allowed quietly to market the oil and mineral products of Almazuvelireksport (precious metals), Raznoimport (nonferrous metals) and Techsnabeksport (rare metals). Senior Kremlin officials, according to sources in the Moscow foreign trade community, were concerned that their profitable relationship with the man who "never asked any questions" might be compromised if any criminal charges against him were to be aired in court. On August 15, 1983, the Moscow daily news-

196

paper *Izvestia* printed a front-page, above-the-fold story blaringly headlined "OPEN BLACKMAIL." The placement of the story held significance, since *Izvestia* and *Pravda* as a rule reserve the front page for domestic news.

"The United States thinks that all countries, big and small, must subvert their national interests to American measures," wrote *Izvestia*'s Zurich correspondent, Vladimir Kuznestov.

"Under the pretext of nonpayment of taxes by the Swiss branch of the Marc Rich firm, American authorities have given an ultimatum: either Switzerland changes its internal legislation or its companies will be deprived of admission to American markets. This action by the Reagan Administration is an open threat, an attempt to interfere into the internal affairs of Western European countries through the threat of economic sanctions. The Americans are living under the illusion of a Pax Americana."

Weinberg recoiled in amazement. What began as a daisy chain had turned into a full-blown international incident. And though his mission was to convict Marc Rich and Pinky Green on a specific set of criminal charges, he couldn't help but wonder just what these guys were really up to. They certainly ran with some powerful chums who didn't want to see the case brought to trial.

Courtrooms, like Hilton hotels and 1957 Chevys, are all pretty much the same: dulled lighting, worn carpets and the bloodshot eyes of court reporters staring listlessly into their machines. Sameness is supposed to be part of America's legal fabric, necessary to keep the republic's courts an impartial forum open to rich and poor alike. The Founding Fathers, however, never anticipated Marc Rich, who as long as he voluntarily paid America $50,000 a day would be allowed to turn an American court into a freak game of hide-and-seek. On August 15, for instance, Weinberg told Judge Sand that Rich had yet to turn over the critical documents he required to bring the Rich case to trial. "These documents would fill a briefcase, Your Honor."

197

"You'd swap the steamer trunks for an attaché case!?!" said the judge.

"Exactly, Your Honor!"

The case was weird, its issues spiraling into fresh tendrils of confusion every day, desensitizing even those who were involved intimately. "I have no idea what Rich wants us to do," one of Rich's lawyers schriptzed. "What the hell you asking me for? I just come to the hearings."

"There was no way we were going to turn over what Weinberg wanted," a former Rich shareholder explained. "The information was worth much more than fifty grand a day . . . information on all our oil deals with Iran. That would have really damaged the company because we were selling Iranian and Soviet oil to South Africa in return for Namibian uranium we sold to the Soviets."

The government claimed that the guilt or innocence of Marc Rich and Pinky Green rested in large part on what was contained in an eighty-three-page ledger that Marc Rich AG, and then the Swiss government, refused to relinquish. But Weinberg's mind-scattering quest for the ledger and other documents had, as Rich planned, obfuscated whether or not he and his partner were guilty of crimes against the United States. The superlatives of money were meaningless to Rich. By the beginning of autumn 1983, Rich and Green had paid their lawyers an estimated $6 million to make it look as if Weinberg was guilty of persecuting them. As attorney Steven Brill, the editor of *The American Lawyer*, pointed out in a scathing editorial directed at the legal profession: "In Rich's case, the lawyers invoked state terror campaigns in Bulgaria and Guatemala as examples of what was likely to happen in America if the government's case against Rich went unchecked."

Rich's lawyers had also spent hours arguing over what legally constituted a secret document; how much time it would take for Marc Rich to "package and box" documents and, if the Swiss decided to "permit" Rich to release them, who would be liable if the plane carrying them crashed en route from

Zurich. During one such courtroom discussion between the defense and the prosecution, a fuming and frustrated Judge Sand barked at one of Rich's lawyers: "We are not dealing with a mom and pop grocery store. We are dealing with a worldwide commodity trader which engages in financial transactions involving literally billions of dollars, using telexes, telephones and all the modern devices for communication. I really do not understand why such an organization could not cause to be brought to the one central location every document called for by its subpoenas, whether these documents are now in Paris, Berlin or Timbuktu."

Weinberg had no intention of waiting to get his hands on documents still in Switzerland before lodging the indictment against Rich, Green and their various doppelgängers. In September 1983 Weinberg let loose his indictment against Marc Rich, Pinky Green, Marc Rich International, Marc Rich AG, Clarendon Limited and Listo Petroleum oil trader Clyde Meltzer. Arco buttressed the case against Rich and Green by supplying the grand jury with information on its 1980 deals for Rich's Nigerian and Angolan crude. Other information was turned over by Exxon, Mobil and Shell, as well as by many of the Rich traders who had had jail sentences dangled in front of them. It was an intimidating broadside.

The original fifty-six-page, fifty-one-count (fourteen further counts would be tacked on later) indictment charged Rich and Green with personally orchestrating racketeering, mail and wire fraud, tax evasion, conspiracy and trading with the enemy. A separate list charged Marc Rich International and Marc Rich AG with forty-one counts of racketeering, racketeering conspiracy and mail and wire fraud. Weinberg hit Rich with a close-quarter burst of legal buckshot, riddling him with charges of everything from using the United States Post Office's Express Mail Service to mail false profit statements to devising secret telex codes to transmit the details of treasonous deals with the Ayatollah Ruhollah Khomeini.

Weinberg contended that all this, and more, was part of a

199

spectacular fandango between Marc Rich AG and Marc Rich International to avoid paying taxes. The government alleged that in 1980 alone, Rich ladled at least $20 million in taxable cash into his offshore pots. Listo Petroleum and West Texas Marketing added to the magnitude of the deal by purchasing $300 million of crude oil directly from Marc Rich AG—a blatant contradiction of Marc Rich's personal assurance that his Swiss company did no business in the United States.

The indictment alleged that over a nine-month period in 1980, Marc Rich International bought $345 million worth of crude oil from Marc Rich AG and sold it at a loss of $110 million. A list of twenty documented transactions was provided in the indictment. In one instance Rich's American company bought Peruvian Loredo crude oil from his Swiss company for $40 a barrel and then—on the same day—resold it to West Texas Marketing for $33.10 a barrel. This was done to create a price gap in deals between New York and Zug in order to give the impression of a loss to avoid paying taxes.

Marc Rich, claimed the U.S. government, had a real talent to scope out deals designed to create tax losses. On December 2, 1979, for instance, Marc Rich International bought 327,063 barrels of Nigerian Bonny light crude from Marc Rich AG at $37 a barrel. Nine days later the crude was resold to Ashland Oil for $22.50 a barrel—a loss of $14.50 a barrel.

The government also hamstrung Rich with a "crude reseller audit" through the Department of Energy's Economic Regulatory Administration. The object of this separate investigation was to discover if Rich and Green closed domestic spot market oil deals through Zug in avoidance of regulations limiting the profit a middleman could make on the oil trades. Though these rules were spiked by the federal government in 1981, Weinberg wanted to nail Rich for the hundreds of millions of dollars he earned from selling Persian oil to the United States during the Iranian hostage crisis. Rich and Green spent upwards of $200 million to purchase Iranian oil during the hostage crisis, giving the Khomeini regime money for oil in violation of the presidential order. The figure didn't take into account the millions Rich spent to purchase arms and spare parts to trade with Khomeini for access to the tanks on Kharg Island.

Rich was liable for $34 million in illegal, hidden profits made through spurious crude oil transactions sculpted to create massive profits on Marc Rich International's books, plus another $71 million in illegal, domestic profits spooned offshore. The millions came from deals hidden through daisy chains linking West Texas Marketing and Listo Petroleum. In one such daisy chain, Rich bought 18 million barrels of Alaskan North Slope oil from Arco. He then told Arco to switch the contract to Listo Petroleum. Listo destroyed documents identifying the oil as controlled oil and forged papers to identify it as uncontrolled oil. Listo then sold it back to Marc Rich at a fraction of the market price, but well above the controlled price.

All profits from the daisy chains were earned in violation of federal law because labels were switched. Since tax returns needed to be filed on the illegal profits, Rich often directed West Texas Marketing and Listo Petroleum to bill Marc Rich International at higher, world market prices for the disguised crude. Rich agreed to kick back the difference between the controlled price and the invoice price. The result of this shuffle was that none of the profits ended up on Marc Rich's American financial ledgers but accumulated in the offshore pot shared with the two Texas companies—$23 million for West Texas Marketing and $47 million for Listo Petroleum between October 1980 and May 1981.

The indictment further charged Rich's Swiss company with selling discounted foreign oil to Charter Oil Company's Bahamian subsidiary while Marc Rich International bought controlled American oil from Charter. The controlled American oil went directly into the West Texas Marketing daisy chain. Rich ordered his comptroller in New York to counterfeit invoices from these deals to make it appear that Marc Rich AG really made the profit on the Charter deals. Original invoices were destroyed and replaced with more authentic-looking AG invoices mailed or couriered from Zug. Yet another $31 million was transferred from New York to Zug by grace of forged and fabricated invoices.

The plunder was moved offshore through deception. Rich's traders were directed to conduct nonexistent deals that sold foreign crude to West Texas Marketing and Listo Petroleum. Hours after these fake trades were put into motion, the two companies would resell the invisible oil to one of Rich's Panamanian companies at a loss of $3 a barrel. There were at least eighteen such bogus transactions—some of which documented Rich's traders placing their invisible oil aboard actual tankers in the middle of the ocean.

Sandy Weinberg made a conservative estimate of the amount Rich owed in back taxes: $96 million. Others on the defense team said that if they could get their hands on the Swiss documents, the figure might double, triple or maybe quadruple. It was the largest known criminal scheme to avoid paying taxes in history.

The United States government issued warrants for the arrest of Marc Rich and Pinky Green on September 19, 1983. Rich and Green were in Zug and had no intention of turning themselves in to the American consul thirty miles away in Zurich. Justice and State Department officials met in Washington to devise a strategy. Since they knew Rich and Green would never willingly come back to the United States, the outlook was bleak. Tax evasion was not an extraditable offense in Switzerland, and there were no solid legal nuances in the extradition treaty signed between Switzerland and the United States in May 1900. The treaty, in fact, was drawn up before America even had an income tax, making the only extraditable offenses arson, murder, armed robbery, embezzlement, forgery, rape, abduction, piracy, perjury and destruction of railroad property. There was an outside chance of convincing the Swiss to return Rich and Green for allegedly forging oil labels, but to do that they would have to prove the charges true and they needed Rich and Green to accomplish that task. "The treaty doesn't include modern crimes," Swiss government attorney Robert Herzstein reminded American Justice Department officials smugly.

The Swiss cabinet drew up a series of measures to protect Swiss interests in any legal dispute with the United States, asserting that American legal proceedings extending onto Swiss territory violated laws of sovereignty. "It's up to Swiss authorities to determine whether Swiss law is violated or not," Swiss attorney Juerg Leutert reminded anyone who asked what Berne intended to do with its American fugitives in Zug. Weinberg didn't care. If the Swiss wanted to protect Rich, Green and the documents, then he would hold off filing for extradition and instead bring Rich's companies to court and levy a "jeopardy assessment" (an action that freezes assets when tax collection may be jeopardized) against Clarendon for $90.4 million. "Rich was gone," said Weinberg. "The case became a matter of money."

The idea of a jeopardy assessment didn't sit well with Rich's attorneys. They still wanted to negotiate some kind of settlement. Ten of Rich's attorneys led by Boris Kostelanetz got together with Weinberg and his team in early October in an attempt to decide what was going to be done about Marc Rich and Pinky Green. "The meetings were totally useless," said one of the lawyers in attendance. "We sat around a table for a couple of days listening to Boris tell us these terrific stories of what it was like trying criminal cases back in the 1920s. I don't think anyone wanted to mention Rich's name. Boris is that good a storyteller."

Rich was obviously ready to pay the price to stay a free man. Weinberg was more than glad to collect, hitting Clarendon with the jeopardy assessment of $90.4 million in back taxes, penalties and interest from thirteen banks doing business with Clarendon. This time it was the bankers who recoiled and asked federal Judge Richard Owen to grant an injunction to block the Internal Revenue Service from col-

203

lecting the cash, arguing that they had first claim to Clarendon's money. Bankers once glad to extend millions in short-
term credit to help finance Marc Rich International's deals
were reeling in shock. Chemical Bank was the first to blackball
International/Clarendon. Manufacturers Hanover and Chase
Manhattan spiked Rich's American loans as well, but Rich—
audacious as ever—had Clarendon ask them to convert his
credit lines into a revolving $250 million line. The banks
nearly acquiesced, but Rich could not provide secure guar-
antees because Weinberg said that all assets belonged to Uncle
Sam. Judge Owen upheld the assessment. Clarendon used
what money it had left in the United States to reduce about
$100 million of its short-term liabilities with the banks. The
long-term figure, totaling $130 million, was guaranteed by
Marc Rich AG but owed by Clarendon to Chase Manhattan
Bank, Bankers Trust Company, Marine Midland Bank, Paris-
Bas, Bank of Boston International, First National Bank of
Boston, Banque Indosuez, French American Banking Cor-
poration, Société Générale, Girard Bank, Swiss Banking Corporation and the First National Bank of Chicago.

Weinberg also caught Rich liquidating $750 million of his
American assets between March and August while trying to
avoid the grand jury probe. Marc Rich International stripped
its total worth from over $1 billion to $261 million over the
first six months of the grand jury investigation. Another $45
million was moved to bank accounts in the Bahamas and the
Cayman Islands during the summer of 1983. Peter Ryan, a
former middle manager for Chase Manhattan Bank who became chief financial officer of Clarendon and president of
Richco Sugar, asserted boldly that "only because of the jeopardy assessment was Clarendon in any peril of insolvency."

By the end of October over forty people had received their
"Pinky" slips, and the remaining 130 employees knew that
their days were numbered. On October 27 Richco Bullion,
Rich's London-based bullion and foreign exchange operation,
withdrew from the game for good. A few days before that,

Richco Capital, Richco Bullion's affiliated dealer in America, shut down because the legal developments destroyed the reputation on which gold deals had to be based. "Everyone who worked for Marc in New York concluded that we were lunch meat by the beginning of the second quarter of 1983," one of the firm's former traders explained. "Marc and Pinky got to go to Switzerland. We went to unemployment."

"The company did try to help find us new jobs," another Rich trader in New York explained, "but all that anyone in the business wanted to talk about was Marc and Pinky. I went in for an interview at Exxon, and the guy who was supposed to interview me had three other people in his office wanting to know if I was involved in the scandal. They didn't care if I was a crook—they wanted to know what Marc was getting away with and who was involved."

Added another Rich trader: "I just stopped going to interviews all together. It was too embarrassing."

Rich and Green, meanwhile, were hiding out in Zug. Fuzzy mug shots and their passport numbers were distributed to every point of entry into the United States. The two men, however, had no intention of returning to America and made provisions to ensure that Weinberg would have a sticky time getting them back through the courts. Although Rich had aligned himself securely with the Swiss, he decided to leave nothing to chance if Weinberg were successful in pressing Berne for extradition. Rich applied for and was quickly granted Spanish citizenship, telling associates that if things got too hot in Zug he could move to Madrid because Spain's extradition deal with the United States said "neither state shall be bound to deliver up one of its nationals."

Pinky Green became a Bolivian.

CHAPTER 17

The race is not always to the swift, nor the battle to the
strong—but that's the way to bet.

DAMON RUNYON

THE TRADERS who traveled to the London Metal Exchange dinner to toast their prodigious wealth on
October 11, 1983, radiated the tawny hues of fear.
It was not Rich's staggering back-tax bill for a handful of questionable oil deals conducted over a few years that
frightened the dinner-jacketed gentlemen. It was that one of
their own had allowed spears of light to be cast on the pen-
ultimate secrets of their lives, to be put on public parade in
the circuslike confines of a Manhattan courtroom.

"Everyone in this business has dealt with Marc Rich," said
a cuticle-chewing broker who had bought and sold millions
of dollars of Rich's wares in the United States and Europe.
"The last thing we want is the United States poring over
records that might outline our activities. We do not want people to understand how we operate."

"It's a numbers game," quipped an American trader who
buries much of his profit in Zug. "Marc would be paying 47
percent in taxes and have the federal government looking up
his ass if he kept his money in America. In Zug he's paying
maybe 10 percent, and the Swiss love him. So which is the

better business deal? That's all it was . . . a better business
deal. So what if he daisy chained oil and traded with Iran?
We're here to make money, not give communion."

Marc Rich's world had been penetrated and his colleagues
were greatly concerned that the ripple effect of the indictment
might also drown them. Even *Metal Bulletin*, usually the un-
abashed cheerleader for the trading profession, presented an
editorial slugged: "RICH—A DAMAGING CASE." It said that although Rich had not suffered materially, the company had
"severely reduced [i.e., decimated] its directly transacted
business in America. As a result some of the coolest brows in
the metal business are now looking distinctly ruffled. The
glare of publicity which has shone on Rich has been about as
welcome as a set of car headlamps to a road-crossing mole."

Mr. Josephson understood the conclave's fears and to calm
them placed a large advertisement on the business news page
of the *International Herald Tribune*. The advertisement read:
"TAX HAVEN BANK . . . Priced for quick sale at $60,000."

Mr. Josephson, a freelance banker who empathized with
the varying fortunes of greed, held court in the bar of Knights-
bridge's Basil Street Hotel, a sleepy place usually frequented
by wealthy American tourists. But the characters who streamed
into the lobby during London Metal Exchange Week were
not Americans in search of the autumn sales at Harrods. They
were metal men afraid of being baked in the peculiar afterglow
of the indictment against Marc Rich and Pinky Green.

"Privacy is the primary purpose of owning a bank," Mr.
Josephson explained while nursing a tall scotch and water.
"The United States does not afford privacy to its citizens.
Whose damn business is it how much money Marc Rich had?
Whose damn business is it how much money anybody in any
business has!"

Mr. Josephson had never had the "good fortune" of meeting
Marc Rich but was in London to feed off his wounds. His
business was disposing of banks, void of any currency or ownership controls, that he had established in the Cayman Islands.

Mr. Josephson's banks were like any other bank, with the ability to issue checks, letters of credit or cash from a street corner money machine. The Cayman Islands, he enthusiastically told the traders who visited him, allowed anyone to open a bank if they could produce initial deposits of $250,000. Once the structure was established, owners like Mr. Josephson could pull out their $250,000 and auction the shell operation to the highest bidder. And bidders from the trading community were gathering in the Basil Street Hotel to listen to Mr. Josephson the way cardinals pour into the Sistine Chapel to elect a new pope.

"It takes too much time to clear checks of hundreds of millions of dollars," Mr. Josephson lectured his customers. "The money is traceable, too. With your own bank you can keep the money working for you and you alone. Buy a Cayman bank and you can create your own impenetrable world."

But there were traders, of course, glad to see Rich's operation being ripped into. Some were jealous of the success that met the company; others, indignant, felt it was due justice for the selfish manner in which Rich often handled commodities that affected their own pockets. Everyone, however, was hungry for the leftovers. As *Metal Bulletin* said shrewdly, "traders have broad smiles on their faces in anticipation of new business opportunities arising as Rich's troubles take their toll."

Marc Rich and Pinky Green still had a lot of life—and money—left in their veins, despite the bloodsuckers lining up to exsanguinate their corporations. Adverse publicity had made Clarendon's future impracticable, so contingency plans were drawn up to establish a clean American base to take the company's place once the legal mess could be cleared up. According to Rich's traders, if a Rich deal-in-progress stood to add to the legal rubble, consumers were asked to make their checks payable to a number, not a name. His offshore bankers comfortably obliged.

Managing affairs from the Zug headquarters or the mansion

atop Himmelreich (Heaven's Empire) in Baar, Rich placed some of International/ Clarendon's $300,000-a-year traders inside other American trading firms. These already existing operations were now Rich client states. One such firm, Trans-World Metals in New York, hired ten former International/ Clarendon traders and was nicknamed "Trans-Rich Metals." Rich traders Alter Goldstein and Dick Schwartz crossed the street to Amalgamet. Although the move was costly because higher commissions had to be paid to move the material through Trans-World and other companies, Marc Rich AG ended 1983 with $15 billion in worldwide sales, of which the American market accounted for $3 billion. Money, of course, was no object. "Scary stuff Rich is doing," said one of the company's changelings in New York. "You keep looking over your shoulder for someone to hand you a subpoena."

A few of Rich's oil traders on the street looking for jobs were upset. They knew that nobody else would pay the kind of money that Rich did and they had become accustomed to the high life. "We also lost the Ariano edge," an out-of-work Rich oil trader complained. "Arco's people used to filter us information on how much other traders were bidding for their domestic crude. That's one of the reasons we did so well. Now we're just like everybody else in the business."

Money due to Rich traders for bonuses and outstanding stock was put on hold, and a carefully couched verbal warning issued from Heaven's Empire: If former employees wanted their money, it would be best not to collaborate with government or journalistic investigations into the company. To press his point Rich asked the federal court to put a gag order on public discussion of the case. The judge refused the motion but added that the Justice Department had come "perilously close" to exceeding its jurisdiction in public statements it had already made.

The court's warning was moot. Rich's attorneys had already bought the American justice system. The speedy trial act— a law requiring that a trial commence between thirty and seventy days after indictment—had been bought by the highest bidder. "When you've got a client who can pay and pay and pay for every argument," said Weinberg, "you just make every argument, no matter how absurd."

Arguments to set a trial date and to drop the charges against Rich, Green and their American business operation continued until March 1984, when the government removed its allegation that Marc Rich International traded with Iran during the hostage crisis. Marc Rich AG responded to the event by closing the world's biggest single export shipment of steel scrap metal. It cost Rich $1 million to move a cargo of 45,000 tons of scrap worth around $5 million from Liverpool, England, to Japan and South Korea. He also closed a deal to have the supertanker *Cougar* carry 280,000 tons of Iranian oil from Kharg Island to the Red Sea.

In late March the Justice Department allowed Rich to sell off items from his American metal inventory, with the revenues placed in a court escrow account. A fire sale it wasn't— Rich sold nearly 1 million pounds of material at full market price through "Trans-Rich Metals." The broker was John Erickson, who had previously spent eight years with Rich in New York. Clarendon's opulent offices in the Piaget Building were nearly deserted. "The Marc Rich name has become somewhat of a liability," said Inner Circle member Willi Strohotte, commenting on Clarendon. "It's become a commercial necessity to make a dissociation." Some 200 people had separated from Clarendon. The only ones left were owner Willi Strohotte, managing director Alexander Hackel, financial manager Peter Ryan, former Listo Petroleum daisy chainer Clyde Meltzer, and a few secretaries. Three blocks away at Philipp Brothers, the mood toward Marc Rich wavered between heartfelt pity and deep scorn. "His name was mentioned only once at a board meeting. Of course Jesselson wasn't in the room," said a director of Phibro-Salomon. "We really didn't say much about him. A couple of guys honestly felt sorry for what happened to him. It must of been dreadful on his family. Everyone shook their heads, you know, because it didn't come as a real surprise . . . what a dumb bastard he was to create such a mess."

Oil wildcatter Marvin Davis, who had bought Twentieth Century-Fox with Rich in 1981, was most likely calling his partner much worse than bastard. Davis wanted to buy out Rich's shares in TCF Holdings and asked the Securities and Exchange Commission permission to do so, but the court wouldn't let Rich sell as long as the case remained unsettled. "Twentieth Century-Fox is forbidden to make or suffer any sale, assignment, transfer or interference with any property in which Marc Rich + Co. AG has an interest up to the amount of $27.5 million," read the government's order. Although Rich's interest was worth more, Weinberg said that the order effectively prevented Rich from selling his Fox shares. Davis, according to a source close to both men, fumed over the court's decision. Fox had lost $17 million on revenues of $152 million for the second quarter of 1983, but by 1984 CBS, ABC and NBC had scheduled eight hours a week of Fox programming for prime time, more than any of the other nineteen independent production companies would have broadcast on network television. Then there was *The Return of the Jedi*—box-office receipts approaching $500 million.

Fox director Henry Kissinger was snoozing fitfully. An article in the Spanish journal *Five Days* alleged that Rich and Kissinger had jointly purchased $200 million worth of the Ayatollah's crude during the hostage crisis, falsified certificates of ownership, and had the funds to purchase the oil transferred to Tehran's control from the Zurich offices of the Swiss Banking Corporation and the Chase Manhattan Bank. Kissinger was awakened by a reporter from *Fortune* magazine who saw him napping in the business-class section on a flight from Paris to London and asked the former secretary of state if he had ever met Rich. The fugitive trader's friend "K" said that he had met Rich only once—at a movie premiere.

A few months after that encounter, the State Department's

Bureau of European Affairs began investigating the actions of America's Vatican ambassador, William A. Wilson, because of his personal intervention into the Rich case; State also launched a separate investigation into his contacts with the Most Reverend Paul C. Marcinkus, the Chicago-born prelate in charge of the Vatican's finances, known as "God's Banker."

Ambassador Wilson traveled under benefit of unique portfolio. He was the only ambassador in American history to be granted an exemption from the policy requiring ambassadors to step down from directorships in profit-making companies. Wilson claimed that he had been permitted to retain his corporate positions because they would not interfere with his ambassadorial duties and because he was not receiving payment for his services. Ambassador Wilson, a longtime friend of Ronald Reagan who served for many years as a trustee of Reagan's finances, was a member of the boards of Penzoil, a company Marc Rich had done business with, and Earle M. Jorgensen Company, a California steelmaker that had need of Rich's metallic additives. On December 12, 1983, then-Undersecretary of State Lawrence S. Eagleburger—Kissinger's longtime political sidekick who is now president of the consulting firm Kissinger Associates—sent a telegram to Ambassador Wilson that is believed to have included a warning that his actions were a source of embarrassment to the Reagan Administration. Ambassador Wilson never revealed what he had spoken about with Rich. All he ever said about the meeting was that he had "reported in full to Larry Eagleburger." The State Department seemed satisfied.

"I think the boys got together to talk a deal," said a Justice Department official, "and they got caught."

The first real authorized rumbles of settlement were in May 1984, when Edward Bennett Williams flew to New York to "get the ball rolling again." Rich had successfully gambled that the Swiss would refuse to extradite him. It was almost a sure bet: Berne had sent a diplomatic note to the State Department pledging to give up the documents if Weinberg dropped his subpoena requesting them, hinting that Switzerland wouldn't play ball with a government that was forcing them onto the field. Rich had assurances from his contacts in Berne that Weinberg would never go along with the deal, because dumping the subpoena would set a precedent that could strip the United States of the right to issue subpoenas in future cases.

Although Switzerland's efforts in support of Rich were not, strictly speaking, a matter of preserving the country's famed banking secrecy laws, they did risk infecting the tissue that protects Swiss-based financial operations from scrutiny. Formally the Swiss refused to assist with the extraterritorial application of United States law. At the core of the issue was landlocked Switzerland's real economic need to remain a haven for white-collar criminals. Weinberg and all the lawyers Rich had hired to sit across from him in the courtroom knew damned well that the Swiss would never adjust to the changing circumstances of the international marketplace. One of Weinberg's long-term shots at snaring Rich and Green would be made possible by the Swiss Parliament's passing a regulation requiring that Swiss banks have their American customers sign a special waiver to divulge certain information to United States authorities. But even that pending bill had a wonderful bit of small print on its bottom. It would be up to an ad hoc committee of Swiss attorneys to first see if the United States indeed had a case that needed to be answered. Since nearly every lawyer in Switzerland sits on the corporate board of some foreign company, the bill would become yet another layer of protection and, for Rich's attorneys, another technique they could wave—like the $19 million worth of $50,000-a-day fines Rich had paid the government from June 1981 to August 1984 for withholding records from a federal grand jury—in front of the court to stall for time.

Sandy Weinberg, frustrated by his case against Rich's corporations being successfully postponed by the defense for the fifth time, formally asked the Swiss to extradite Marc Rich and Pinky Green on July 27, 1984. He used the only ammo left: He compared the fraud and racketeering charges to forgery, the only extraditable item included in the treaty and the only charges contained in the fifty-one-count indictment that Rich and Green could now be tried for under international law. It was now up to the Swiss to react to the request. Swiss justice officials got in touch with Weinberg's office a few weeks later. It was unacceptable. The extradition request had been written in English. Please refile the request in German. There was no end to the madness.

Rich's lawyers had made a $75 million offer to settle the case in January 1984. When Weinberg refused the defense upped the ante to $150 million. Weinberg said no again because, if the government accepted the money, then Rich, under American tax laws, could take a $40 million tax credit on the payoff. Justice Department sources also indicated that Rich and Green wanted immunity from prosecution as part of any settlement package. Weinberg didn't like the sound of the Zug overture and said that he would make no bargains with Rich and Green unless it would "expose them to substantial prison terms."

Back in Zug Rich and Green were more popular than William Tell, more folk hero than fugitive. Rich's only public statement was broadcast over Swiss radio. Asked if he had good contacts with his Swiss neighbors, he answered: "Not yet. Most people who want to have contact with me are reporters or photographers." To show his love of Switzerland, Rich also tried to arrange a controlled press conference with Zurich reporters, but thought it might be wise to first numb them at a huge banquet in a private function room at one of Zurich's swishest restaurants. Rich's Swiss advisors, however, shuddered over throwing a lavish free-for-all feast for journalists, no matter how friendly they appeared, and convinced him to host instead a low-key dinner and discussion for four Swiss reporters in the boardroom of the Volksbank. "Rich didn't say anything of importance," said Fredy Haemmerli, an editor and reporter for the Swiss business magazine *bilanz*. "He thought a dinner with the Swiss press would help. It didn't. He struck me as someone who was always good with the girls, a real lady's man. J. R. Ewing." Zugerlanders were enthralled with the parallels between Marc Rich and J. R. Ewing and even named Rich's blue-glass corporate headquarters the Dallas Building. But the cracks were beginning to show.

Pinky Green longed for Brooklyn; Denise Rich was growing increasingly irritated over her own self-imposed exile, so embarrassed over what was happening to her husband that when she did travel to New York, she failed to contact any of her old friends. Rich and Green also started snapping at each other in the office, something they had never done before. Pinky began complaining about the lack of good kosher food in the foggy Swiss town, so Rich, in response to Pinky's hunger and his own love of eating, opened up the Glashof (Glass House) kosher restaurant across the alley from their headquarters. The dining area was painted dazzling red and filled with mirrors and chrome chairs. Opening night featured an all-female steel band. Zug's other restaurateurs found humor in Rich's selection of a name. But nobody threw any stones. "I think the next thing Zug does is put a statue of Marc and Pinky down by the lake," laughed Urs Rothmayr, owner of Schiff, one of Zug's lakeside restaurants.

Although Rich rarely complained about life in his golden cage, he did want to come back to America but knew that if he did Weinberg would try to put him in jail. The situation was such that Rich's only option was to attempt a final settlement in regards to the charges against his companies. The settlement discussed between his lawyers and the government would not affect the tax-fraud and other criminal charges against him and Green as individuals. The bell signifying the final round of the international tug-of-war sounded in September 1984, when Switzerland formally rejected the Justice Department's request for extradition. The Swiss had said that the fraud charges and tax violations against Rich and Green

215

A. CRAIG COPETAS

were not covered by the extradition treaty and that matters
were complicated by the fact that Rich was now Spanish and
Spain does not extradite its citizens for the evasion of American taxes.

On October 10, 1984, Marc Rich AG, Marc Rich International and Clarendon Limited all pleaded guilty to thirty-eight
counts of tax evasion, $50 million in illegal oil profits in 1980
and 1981 and making false statements to the United States
government. Former Listo Petroleum trader Clyde Meltzer
pleaded guilty to one count of making a false statement about
his oil deals. Clarendon pleaded guilty to two extra counts of
tax evasion. Fugitives Rich and Green still faced charges of
racketeering, fraud, tax evasion and trading with the enemy.

It cost Marc Rich $340 million to get off the hook, not
including interest and lost revenues that pushed the real losses
close to $1 billion. He paid $150 million in government fines
stemming from the guilty plea; $21 million in fines paid since
June 1983 at a rate of $50,000 a day; $780,000 in fines on the
charges; $33,000 in court costs; and some $10 million in legal
fees to his attorneys. The United States also withheld nearly
$37 million in cash of seized Marc Rich assets. Marc Rich AG
also repaid debts of $130 million to fourteen creditor banks
led by Chase Manhattan and agreed to forfeit the right to use
the $150 million payment as a tax liability—which could have
amounted to some $24 to $40 million in write-offs. Clyde
Meltzer was handed a suspended three-year sentence and was
placed on five years' probation. The probation officer was
directed to assign his charge some form of "community service
work."

Rich never admitted to any wrongdoing, but a public statement issued from Himmelreich said that he had agreed to the
settlement "for alleged offenses against the United States tax
laws and against energy regulations which have meanwhile
been repealed even though a lengthy trial probably would
have resulted in a considerably smaller amount . . . the financial strength of the companies remains intact." A few days

after the statement, a Zug trader claimed that Rich was boasting that he could trade himself out of the "situation" in ten weeks. Braggadocio or staggering truth, the money didn't even dent his business. And as long as he stayed in Switzerland, he was safer than Heidi's goats.

Rich and Green were immersed in planning their American corporate comeback even before the settlement was made official. Rich had hired metal marketing whiz Kent Hoffman from Kidd Creek Mines in Toronto to act as a consultant in the reorganization. Initial plans called for Marc Rich International/Clarendon to build a new American headquarters in Stamford, Connecticut, with Willi Strohotte in command. According to Rich executives, one option under serious consideration was for Rich to create smaller trading units structured to reflect being owned by individual Rich traders, but actually controlled by Rich from Zug. There would be little trouble in finding a new batch of fresh recruits because many trading houses had reduced their staffs, creating a reservoir of experienced out-of-work traders.

The only problem Rich and Green had was movement. Even with all their wealth, they were banana republicans unable to leave Switzerland without running the dangerous risk of being detained by a government willing to turn them over silently to the United States. It was the crowning irony of their lives: Marc Rich and Pinky Green used by a government as a tradeable, political commodity with the United States. "I think when your company is headed by a fugitive from justice, you're going to have a little trouble doing business," a senior metal-trading executive from Philipp Brothers said. "It's too risky dealing with a fugitive."

Emotionally, Weinberg acquiesced to the deal because it kept Rich and Green wanted men; realistically, any prosecution on the charges would have taken as long as five years, and had Clarendon been convicted of tax evasion, it would have been entitled to use its payment as a deduction against taxes. Weinberg had obtained more money for the Treasury

217

Department than his team had originally expected to obtain. The outcome was a huge success —the largest settlement for criminal tax evasion in United States history.

The payoff went down on the morning of October 11, in the federal courthouse on Foley Square. "It was like an E. F. Hutton commercial," said federal prosecutor Martin Auerbach, who, along with Morty Dick, was the only member left on Weinberg's team. "Twenty lawyers in a room. Marvin Davis's lawyer handed Rich's lawyer a $116 million check for Twentieth Century-Fox, Rich's lawyer handed a $130 million check for the money they owed the banks and Chase Manhattan's lawyer handed Weinberg a check for $133,081,306.76."

"It was real dramatic and very quiet," Auerbach, who before joining the Justice Department was an attorney at one of the corporate law firms Rich would later put on his payroll, added in a tired voice. "All anyone could do was gawk when the checks were signed over. Imagine what it takes to keep twenty lawyers' mouths shut.

"You know, if I could have asked Rich one question it would have been, 'How do you manage to make money legally?' Who are these guys?"

"Listen," Sandy Weinberg chortled, the Chattanooga drawl stretching across his office. "I'm not gonna tell ya what I said when we made a deal for money instead of Marc and Pinky. I wanted those boys in jail. But they can't come back into the United States as free men. Never. Those indictments are outstanding . . . no statute of limitations . . . and Marc and Pinky will try to come back. Bet on it."

EPILOGUE

Thou call'dst me a dog before thou hadst a cause,
But since I am a dog, beware my fangs.

Shylock, Act III, Scene iii,
WILLIAM SHAKESPEARE, *The Merchant of Venice*

LUDWIG JESSELSON tinkers with his gold watch fob and then straightens the milky pearl pin holding a dark blue tie to his neatly pressed white shirt. He stands up from behind his desk and greets the visitor with a remarkably vigorous handshake for a man of seventy-five years, a result, he says, of twice yearly ski trips and golf whenever time permits.

"How are you?" the visitor asks.

"I am getting old, young man," he says, the handshake falling away.

"They are all gone," he says a few moments later, his head arching back to point out the framed photographs of Siegfried Ullmann, Siegfried Bendheim and Oscar Philipp. His tone is not morose, just the timbre of a man who has seen everything there is to be seen and is growing tired.

His office staff are caught in a time warp; the men smoke Camels and the women prance between desks on practical pumps. The white Van Heusen shirts and well-sprayed beehive hairdos give the place the look of a fifties rotogravure advertisement. The coffee arrives in china and the sugar is bowled not packeted. Some might complain that the atmosphere here is too mired in tradition for a company that has quarterly net earnings of $120 to $192 million, but the visitor senses that the people who work here care more for each other than yearly sales in the $30 billion range.

Jesselson tells the visitor that Philipp Brothers' association with Engelhard Minerals & Chemicals ended in 1981. "You cannot do justice to an industrial complex if you want to do trading at the same time," he says. "You need to do one thing in order to do it well." The visitor recalls that Philipp Brothers did extremely well: 90 percent of the $10.2 billion of renevue produced by the corporation in its last year of existence was created through lucrative oil, metal and commodity trades masterminded by Ludwig Jesselson and his Philipp Brothers traders during the height of the energy crisis.

The encompassing industrial and financial might of Phibro-Salomon, the holding company that currently owns the trading house Philipp Brothers and the investment banking and securities firm Salomon Brothers, has made the corporation first in U.S. investment bank underwritings, the largest spot oil trading outfit in the world, the most innovative offerer of collateralized mortgage bonds, and the biggest metal-trading company in the history of the business. The reason for all this, and more, is Ludwig Jesselson, who, having run the company on his own between 1964 and 1975, now stands in his corner office as the chairman of Philipp Brothers and the executive vice president of Phibro-Salomon, studying the panorama of New York City with the visitor on a sunny afternoon.

The office next door is empty for the moment. David Tendler, handpicked by Jesselson to run Philipp Brothers, had been edged out by John Gutfreund of Salomon Brothers after a Jesselson-inspired plan failed to take Phibro-Salomon's non-oil commodity business private through a leveraged buy-out. Tendler was a great trader who embodied the Philipp Brothers tradition, but he was—depending on the point of view—a poor manager: He couldn't respond to sinking profits by throwing employees off the ship. "David understood that the staff needed to be cut," said a member of the Phibro-Salomon board sadly. "He was unable to do it. He knew everybody there and couldn't face seeing them on the street. It wasn't the Philipp Brothers way." Philipp Brothers had changed. Their greatest fear had come true: Business-schooled bankers who didn't even know how to write letters of credit had taken over the company. And as Jesselson's freckled hand points out the young men scurrying for success in the concrete canyon below, the soupy light of a late Manhattan summer oozes out from behind a building and, for a moment, fixes a smoldering glow on him, the frail king of an industrial empire now run by writ of minister.

"I still give advice," Jesselson says, returning to the high-backed leather chair behind his desk. "I tell them to never do anything in business that they would not do in their private lives. I built the company on that basis. A good trader needs imagination, an analytical mind, and I gave them room to make mistakes. A trader can never negotiate in fear."

"What's different about the business today?" the visitor asks.

Jesselson closes his eyes and patiently adjusts the black horn-rimmed glasses on his nose. "Patience," he says, eyes opening, the word coming out of his mouth slowly, sorrowfully. "Young traders today don't have the patience to sit around for five years and learn the business. Now we have specialists for every metal. In my day I taught traders to be specialists in everything traded . . . they want it all right now, you know. It's our own fault. We gave them too much money. We made millionaires out of people who anywhere else would have been lucky to make $500 a week.

"It was a mistake," he says quietly, regretfully, the words spilling out as if to apologize for a terrible error that can never be repaired. "We spoiled them."

"Did you spoil Marc Rich?" the visitor inquires.

Jesselson pauses. His eyes swell, then melt into waxy cres-

221

cents. A phone rings and Jesselson pays no attention to the sound. Someone outside answers. Seconds go by and the visitor feels it necessary to invade the silence.

"Where did you go wrong with Marc Rich?" the visitor asks again. "I'm told that you didn't mind his leaving, just the way he did it."

Returning from his deep thought and wiping a speck of something from under his right eye, Jesselson hardens, a visibly emotional old man suddenly transformed into a gut-fighting trader who has just discovered that somebody is positioned to whup him on a deal.

"I will not talk about . . ." Jesselson hesitates and does not mention the name of the man who was once his friend, the *lehrling* he once called son. The force of his voice subsides and his face contorts into conflicting signals: hatred, revenge, sadness finally.

"I will not talk about him," he says like the icy boss of a major multinational corporation who knows that the man in question is his chief competitor.

Jesselson swivels slightly in his chair, and the visitor notices a fleeting glance taken at the photos behind his desk, sun shafts dancing dustily on their fine roan frames.

"He is gone," Jesselson mumbles, like a fragile old man reminded of something that was very precious and lost to him long, long ago.

ACKNOWLEDGMENTS

To THOSE INDIVIDUAL TRADERS around the world who allowed me to conduct deals under their supervision so that I could better grasp the trader's life, I thank you for trusting me to handle your business activities with discretion. Many of those traders who helped me most have no desire to be thanked. They were usually the most helpful. So thank you anyway. You know who you are.

Among those both inside and outside the international commodity trading profession who did help, my sincere gratitude goes to Robert Karl Manoff, Lee Mason, James Horwitz, Grainne James, Constance Sayre, Gerry Joe Goldstein, Christine Goldstein, David Noonan, Susan Faiola, Gary Redmore, Ellen Hume, Terry O'Neil, Calliope, Alan Flacks, Hank Fisher, Ernie Torriero, Gordon "Mr. Rhodium" Davidson, Steve Bronis, Jan Bronis, Steve Shipman, Henry Rothschild, David Tendler, John Leese, Dan Baum, Bert Rubin, Ernie Byle, Steven English and the Cobalt Cartel, Michael Buchter, Peter Marshall, Herve Kelecom, Misha, Mark Heutlinger, Bonnie Cutler, John and Galina Mariani, Bennie (Bollag) and his Jets, Fredy Haemmerli, Wil Oosterhout, Christopher Clark, Eddie de Werk, Hubert Hutton, Fred Schwartz, Ira Sloan, Frank Wolstencroft, Congressman James Santini, John Culkin, Urs Aeby, Lynn Grebstad, Intertech Resources, the Kaypro Corporation, *Harper's* magazine, Cambridge Metals, Redco Resources, the Swire Group, ITR International, Philipp Brothers, the Heavy Metal Kids and . . .

Lynne Murphy, Ludwig Jesselson, Joan Sanger, Esther Newberg.

Particularly Robbie Lichtenstern—who did not live to see this book completed.

Especially W. Douglass Lee, Jr., who by making me his *lehrling*, spent hundreds of hours patiently teaching me how to trade.

Most of all, Jayne Gould.

ABOUT THE AUTHOR

A. Craig Copetas is a journalist who has been an editor at *Esquire* and a writer at *Harper's*, where this book originated as a cover story. He is currently a senior writer for *Inc.* magazine. He was born in Pittsburgh, Pennsylvania, has traveled throughout the world and lives in New York City.